The Entrepreneur's Guide Series

EMPLOYEE MATTERS

A Legal Guide To Hiring, Firing &
Setting Employee Policies

E. Kenneth Snyder

PROBUS PUBLISHING COMPANY
Chicago, Illinois

Library of Congress Cataloging in Publication Data Available

ISBN 1-55738-239-5

Printed in the United States of America

IPC

1 2 3 4 5 6 7 8 9 0

Contents

PREFACE
    vii

1 EMPLOYEE HANDBOOKS   1
Common Law Employee at Will   2
"Handbook" Litigation   4
Strategies to Preserve the Terms and Conditions of
    Employment   8
Conclusion   10

2 RETALIATORY DISCHARGE   11
Consequences of Retaliatory Discharge   11
Cases Defining Retaliatory Discharge   13
Interpretation of the Courts   14
What Can Employers Do to Protect Themselves?   19
Conclusion   19

3 EMPLOYEE WORK RECORDS   21
Law of Defamation Defined   22
How the Law of Defamation Works   23
Strategies to Avoid Legal Liability   24
Conclusion   30

4   EMPLOYEE NONCOMPETITION AGREEMENTS   31
    Intangible Assets   33
    Policy of the Law   35
    Drafting, Negotiating and Enforcing   36
    Geographic and Time Restrictions   37
    The Employer's Existing Legitimate Interests at the Time of
        Termination   38
    Conclusion   41

5   ORGANIZATIONAL RISK MANAGEMENT   43
    Legal Responsibility of Business Enterprises   44
    Legal Liability of Employees While Performing Duties
        for the Corporation   46
    Insurance Coverage   49
    Liability Insurance   53
    Worker's Compensation   54
    Conclusion   56

6   ON-THE-JOB STRESS   57
    Eligibility for Worker's Compensation   58
    Conclusion   65

7   DRUG AND ALCOHOL TESTING   67
    Constitutional Rights of Employment Relationships   71
    Precautions to Avoid Potential Liability   74
    Conclusion   77

8   SMOKING   79
    Smokers' Rights   79
    Employers' Rights   80
    Protecting the Rights of Nonsmokers   81
    Cases Dealing with Smoking   83
    Negligent and Intentional Infliction of Emotional Distress   86
    Conclusion   88

9   AN INTRODUCTION TO ANTIDISCRIMINATION
     LAW   89
     State and Federal Law   90
     Administrative Agencies   93
     Strategies to Protect Management from Discrimination
       Charges   97

10 AGE DISCRIMINATION   101
     Federal and State Law   101
     Mandatory Retirement   106
     Bona Fide Occupational Requirements   106
     Conclusion   108

11 DISABILITY DISCRIMINATION   109
     The Americans with Disabilities Act   110
     State Laws   114
     State Court Precedents   115
     Conclusion   117

12 RELIGIOUS DISCRIMINATION   119
     State and Federal Law   119
     Balancing Work Schedules with Religious Holidays   122
     Conclusion   126

13 RACE DISCRIMINATION   127
     State and Federal Law   128
     Requirements of the Law   130
     Conclusion   134

14 SEX DISCRIMINATION   135
     Laws of Sex Discrimination   136
     Determining Whether Sex Discrimination Exists   139
     Conclusion   143

15 SEXUAL HARASSMENT   145
    State and Federal Law   146
    Sexual Harassment Defined   147
    Obligations of Employers   148
    Other Requirements That Claimant Must Demonstrate   151
    Considerations of Claimant   152
    Conclusion   154

16 MARITAL STATUS DISCRIMINATION   155
    Ground-Breaking Cases   156
    Antinepotism Rules   158
    Husbands and Wives   158
    State Laws   160
    Conclusion   161

17 PREGNANCY DISCRIMINATION   163
    Supreme Court Rulings   164
    EEOC's Guidelines   166
    Leading Cases Which Interpreted the Law   168
    Conclusion   172

INDEX   175

Preface

The focus of *Employee Matters* is to outline how employers can avoid employment-related litigation or, if unavoidable, how employers can minimize the damage and maximize their chance of winning. This book will acquaint anyone who holds a position of some responsibility in a small-business, corporate, or other organizational setting with the basic underlying legal themes in a number of areas on personnel management. All of the common areas of contention in litigation involving employers and employees are covered. Hopefully the reader will come away with a very fundamental and at the same time rather sophisticated understanding of how to set policies and implement procedures for effective personnel risk management. It is almost inevitable that every employer will realize the need for this information at one time or another, but, unfortunately, once suit has been filed it is really too late use it effectively. Effective management of litigation risks starts at the policy-planning phase and must be implemented in the employer's day-to-day dealings with each and every employee.

The approach taken in this book is not to create a legal "cookbook" with complicated recipes or to concoct a "how-to" book with simplistic home remedies spoon-fed to the legally uninitiated. *Employee Matters* concentrates on explaining the most important principles in a way the intelligent, but legally untrained reader will find illuminating and useful.

All the material is important and it is best, if possible, to read the whole book from start to finish. However, I also have tried to accommodate the reader who will want to jump right in to chapters dealing with matters of immediate or pressing concern. The book is organized so that the simplest and most basic issues are handled in the earliest chapters. The material becomes increasingly more complex as the reader moves toward the middle and the end of the book. The order of the chapters, thus, is not meant to suggest which areas of employment law are the most important, relevant, or necessary, just which are best to tackle first before going on to more challenging material.

EMPLOYEE MATTERS

fact pattern which gave rise to the employee's grievances. Once they are in court, there is often nothing management and its legal counsel can do to change an unfavorable result. The decision of the court at that point will be based largely on what has already happened, what actually transpired to give rise to the employee's grievance, and whether that pattern of conduct was one for which the law will offer legal redress.

The important task in formulating sound personnel policies is for personnel policy makers to gain a solid understanding of the dynamics of the legal issues involved and to carry out sound and effective planning of policies formulated around an understanding of these issues. This will minimize exposure to litigation and maximize management's chances of winning if the case does end up in the courtroom.

When considering employee handbooks from this perspective, the most salient consideration is to try to avoid having the provisions of the handbook become a binding employment contract between management and its employees. To understand why this is vitally important, it is necessary to understand the basics of what the law presumes the employment relationship is to entail in the absence of a binding employment contract.

Common Law Employee at Will

If there is no contract of employment between the employer and the employee, the law in the United States is that the employee is considered a common law employee at will. Being an employee at will means that the employee can quit at any time, for any reason, and the employer can discharge the employee at any time, for any reason. Of course, employment at will is only an abstract legal concept used in analyzing the employment relationship from an historical perspective. There are so many factors in modern employment law that pure employment at will as it was in the eighteenth century does not really exist anymore.

The most important modern exception to employment at will is employment discrimination law, which is treated extensively later in this book. Whether or not there is an employment contract, an employee cannot be discharged, or be subject to discipline or to modification of the terms and conditions of employment, in any situation where a motivating factor is discrimination based on race, religion, age, gender, marital status, national origin, pregnancy and, in some contexts, sexual or political orientation.

The present discussion also assumes that the employer/employee is not operating in a context covered by a labor/management collective bargaining agreement, in force or under negotiation.

Collective bargaining agreements are colloquially referred to as "contracts," but they are not contracts at all in the strict legal sense, and they are not what is meant by an employment contract when the term is used here or later in the section on personnel management and employment law. Where there is a collective bargaining agreement in force, the agreement governs the relationship between management and labor. The employee handbook, if there is one, would have little actual import aside from the controlling provisions of the collective bargaining agreement.

Of course, states and the federal government have wage-and-hours legislation and occupational safety and health statutes and regulations which set very basic minimum standards in the areas which these laws cover. The provisions of these laws are mandatory and are not subject to negotiation or modification by agreement between management and workers. In fact, trying to induce workers to give up their rights in these contexts can be treated as criminal offenses in some jurisdictions.

Assuming discrimination has not occurred or other special legal rights enjoyed by employees have not come into play, the argument goes that if the employee and employer are at all times free to end the employment relationship for any reason, they are each likewise free to modify it at any time to better suit their individual needs. Or they are free to take advantage of their shifting strengths and weaknesses in negotiating postures.

Simple dissolution of the relationship is always the ultimate recourse if the parties are unable to come to an acceptable working agreement. In the main, when dealing with wages, hours, benefits, and work rules, there is nothing wrong with management or workers changing the terms and conditions of employment at any time they choose, or terminating the employment relationship at any time they see fit, for any reason whatsoever. Employees are commonly thought to enjoy the freedom to quit at any time, to move on to another job, go back to school, retire, or to do whatever else they want. Since they can quit any time they want, they are free at any time to demand raises, better working conditions, or whatever else they want, with the ultimate bargaining card being their option to move on to greener pastures if negotiations are not fruitful.

Employers, on the other hand, are commonly thought to be bound to provide not only employment, wages, and benefits but opportunities for promotion and salary advancement to their employees, as long as the employees choose to stay with them.

But this is just not the case legally. Employers are as free to modify the terms and conditions of employment, or to end it, as employees are. Preservation of this freedom from judicial modification and from the threat of liability for damages in court after the fact, if permissible and feasible, is the import of this chapter.

The basic rule is that employers are free to dictate the terms and conditions of employment where discrimination, collective bargaining, basic wage-and-hour, safety, and health laws are not concerned. Employees are free to accept these conditions, negotiate with their employers to get them to dictate more favorable terms, or quit and leave. This is what is now meant by common law employment at will.

"Handbook" Litigation

However, courts in many U.S. jurisdictions do not like the employment at will doctrine. Case precedents in these jurisdictions have begun to fashion what is coming to be known as the "handbook" exception to the rule of employment at will. The provisions of employee handbooks are taken to modify the at-will status of the relationship between employers and employees, and they create what amounts to be binding contracts requiring both sides to be bound by the terms of the employee handbook.

Since the employer is free to dictate the actual terms which will go into the handbook, this apparent judicial attitude toward limiting the employer's prerogatives (with respect to at-will employment) would seem not to present a problem which the employer could easily circumvent. But in actual practice, there are problems for management who are not wary about how their employee handbooks are put together.

The principal problem is that employers are being held by the courts to be legally bound to abide by the terms of policies they set out in their handbooks. Employers often thought, when formulating the policies and writing the handbooks, that these conditions would only apply unilaterally to their employees. This is exactly the opposite of what was meant to be.

Just Cause

The most common theme which has surfaced in "handbook" litigation is one where the handbook reserves management the right to terminate any employee at any time for "just cause," despite whatever seniority rights the employee may have or other aspects of the employee's status within the organization. This seems innocuous enough on its face, at least until its full significance is appreciated.

The courts in some U.S. jurisdictions are finding that a just-cause termination provision in an employee handbook means that the employee can *only* be terminated for just cause. Leaving aside for the moment the question of defining "just cause," it should be obvious that this sort of judicial interpretation of a relatively common provision of most employee handbooks turns the whole employment at-will doctrine completely upside down.

If an employee can be fired only for "just cause," then the employee is essentially guaranteed employment with the company, without diminution of salary or benefits, as long as the employee chooses to stay. Any major downward modification of the employee's salary, benefits, or status within the organization could be treated as "constructive" termination, that is, trying by more subtle means to force the employee to quit rather than coming right out and firing the person. Constructive termination would also be forbidden, under this logic, unless the employer can demonstrate that "just cause" exists.

If the employer is not careful, the employer will be bound to offer continued employment to individuals whom the employer may not wish to keep around. The employer might not be able to modify the relationship with the workforce when economic conditions might allow the employer to strike a better deal, from the employer's perspective, than was struck when the employee in question came on board.

If an employee can be discharged for "just cause," and only for that reason, then the employer is left wondering exactly what "just cause" entails. Each controversy with each employee will become a separate battleground. The rules of the engagement will not be known or actually defined, possibly until the matter has already been resolved by a particular judge in civil court, according to that judge's view of the law. Is "just cause" defined from the employer's perspective, to effectuate the employer's prerogatives, or is it defined from the standpoint of what the employees need and desire?

The employer needs to maximize return on invested capital by creating an efficiently organized work environment where everyone conforms with the accepted management strategy, whatever that happens to be, so that the constantly changing needs of the relevant market can be met on a expeditious basis. People who are economically redundant, who do not produce, who do not fit in, or who get in the way have to go.

Employees, on the other hand, have always wanted to maximize the value of the return for their labor and maintain job security, at least as long as they choose to remain with the company. In addition, they are now seen as having intangible needs such as status and acceptance within the organizational community which some feel deserve to be recognized.

In defining the parameters of "just cause" the courts have no easy task, and predicting how a particular court will define this term is very speculative, to say the least. It is best not to get into the argument in the first place, perhaps by leaving "just cause" out of the employee handbook, or by defining it so that it refers only to factors which, in the judgment of management, constitute appropriate grounds for termination.

Disciplinary Processes and Procedures

Court precedents on provisions in employee handbooks dealing with disciplinary processes and procedures are also varied. The same sort of turnabout has happened here that took place with provisions for "just cause" termination. Employers have placed language in employee handbooks to delineate what can happen in the event employees' conduct and performances are not up to appropriate standards, only to have the courts interpret the handbooks to set out what must take place before disciplinary sanctions can be imposed.

In many instances the courts have found provisions of handbooks dealing with disciplinary procedures to create basic mandatory procedural safeguards which must be observed before disciplinary measures can be invoked. As an example of how this logic might work, consider the following hypothetical situation. The handbook states that a supervisor can warn an employee for being absent from work twice without a doctor's excuse, a manager can reprimand an employee who has received two warnings from a supervisor, and the head of human resources can fire an employee when the third reprimand would be in order. A court later could conceivably rule that the employee can be fired *only* after all of these steps have taken place, and otherwise the employee has a legal right to continued employment.

Of course it will be more complicated and difficult for the employer than the hypothetical example. The employer will have to demonstrate that each of the preliminary steps was carried out in all fairness, with due regard to the truth of the allegations which precipitated it and without undue intrusion into the decision-making process of personal bias or animosity from the individuals involved.

Employers can unwittingly dedicate large segments of their own and their supervisors' and managers' time, to protracted mock court proceedings in the workplace over disciplinary issues, if the wording and implementation of the employee handbook permits or calls for repeated adjudications of the sort just described.

On the other hand, some courts have actually given the employer the benefit of the doubt in some cases. This occurs where the company has set up grievance procedures which call for appeals of lower level personnel decisions to a "higher court" in upper management, and the employee has run off to file suit in court without going through channels to obtain a final ruling from the "highest court" within the company.

Policies in the employee handbook having to do with benefits, raises, promotions, transfers, advancement, leave, and just about everything else can lead to these same sorts of suits between employees and employers. These policies, set out in the employee handbook as an expression of what management can or might offer to selected employees under appropriate circumstances, may later be taken by the courts as expressions of every employee's inalienable rights in the workplace.

What are private employers, policy-making executives, personnel managers, supervisors and bosses of every stripe to do with respect to employee handbooks? There are several strategies with respect to employee handbooks which have had some measure of success in preserving as much as possible of the employer's prerogatives over control of the terms and conditions of employment.

Strategies to Preserve the Terms and Conditions of Employment

One obvious strategy is not to have an employee handbook at all, or to have one which only contains a lot of "fluff" about the overall organizational mission and company philosophy, but does not get down to brass tacks about the everyday concerns facing employees. One potential strategy, which carries no clear guarantee of success, is to place a disclaimer in the employee handbook. The disclaimer should state that the handbook is only an expression of management policy, and it is not intended to create enforceable rights for the employees. As with legal disclaimers in other commercial contexts, it must be conspicuous enough to draw the average person's attention, and it must be written in language that the average employee can and will understand. It might be appropriate to have the employee sign a statement that he or she understands and agrees that the matters covered in the handbook are only expressions of management policy on those issues, and they are not binding contractual rights benefiting employees. This should be covered before the employee actually starts work, so that it is clear that the employee agreed to the arrangement from the start and that the disclaimer is not a modification of an arrangement which was already in force when the disclaimer was executed.

There is nothing conceptually wrong with a simple and clearly worded disclaimer in the context of an employee handbook as long as it is not an attempt to modify basic rights and responsibilities under wage-and-hours, occupational safety and health, anti-discrimination, unemployment and industrial insurance laws. However, in actual practice, disclaimers of this sort often surface as ineptly drawn "fine print" full of legalistic mumbo-jumbo, which inevitably can be expected to offend the average judge's sense of fair play. If this is the case, the disclaimer will be struck down on whatever grounds can be found to justify the judge's gut reaction against apparent unfairness and overreaching on the employer's part.

Another strategy which might eliminate some of the problems is to have different handbooks distributed at different levels within the organization. Initially, this seems as unfair as having one rule book for umpires and another rule book for the players, but as long as the strategy is implemented competently and effectively there is really nothing wrong with it. Instead of spelling out for all employees as a group the circumstances under which and in what manner they can be disciplined, given raises or promotions, transferred, and the like, it may work out better to give this information only to appropriately placed managers or supervisors. This would seem preferable to writing a handbook which essentially opens up the company's personnel policy file and shares it with the entire rank and file.

In fact, it may work out best that workers are only given very general information about their job titles, when, where, and to whom they are to report to work, and from whom they get their paychecks. In this example, supervisors will only be informed how they are to deal with the workers directly under them. Managers will be informed how to deal with supervisors and how to instruct supervisors in how to deal with workers. Executives will be given similar instruction in dealing with managers, and so on up the chain of command. The theory here is that policies meant only for the eyes of those higher in the company hierarchy cannot create legal rights for, or legal responsibilities toward, those lower down in the organizational structure who are not meant to be privy to expressions of the policies in question.

Employers have had success in court avoiding unwanted legal and contractual responsibilities to their employees with this type of strategy. The problem with it, however, from a management perspective is that it makes the lines of organizational communication very cumbersome. It also promotes rigid distinctions of authority and premises the success or failure of the whole enterprise on the competence and integrity of individual persons or small control groups close to the apex of the organizational pyramid. All of this is at odds with contemporary theories of effective organizational motivation, which feature participatory management and decentralization of authority and decision making.

Some employers might be tempted to throw out their employee handbooks altogether. This action would not do away with or diminish rights which have already come into existence, and may cause more trouble than it is worth after all is said and done. Most employers will have to come to terms with the fact that employee handbooks are a part of life in modern enterprises, at least in companies which are not run personally on a day-to-day basis by their owners, but those which depend on professional business and human resources management.

Conclusion

Employers must realize that employee handbooks are a focus of litigation in our courts which, for better or worse, is right now in the process of establishing that employees do have certain vested rights in their jobs and cannot be dealt with arbitrarily or summarily as they were only a few decades ago. The most prudent course may be to recognize that the most valuable asset of every business enterprise is its people, people who are able and want to do a good and successful job, if properly motivated, managed, and led by those in charge.

Chapter Two

Retaliatory Discharge

The law of retaliatory discharge is a major factor in the current popularity of suits by disaffected employees against their former employers. Retaliatory discharge takes place when an employee is terminated for some type of action or pattern of conduct by the employee which is legally protected from retaliatory action by the employer.

Under the U.S. legal system, employees are considered employees at will, assuming there is no employment contract in force which limits the circumstances under which the employee can be terminated. But the law of retaliatory discharge effectively suspends the rule of employment at will in situations where the courts will find it necessary to protect employees from impermissible retaliatory conduct toward them by their employers.

Consequences of Retaliatory Discharge

When retaliatory discharge can be proven in court, the suit can result in a substantial damage award against the employer. A wrongfully dismissed employee can collect for past and future loss of income, and for injury to the employee's reputation, professional standing, and future earning potential.

Mental anguish and emotional distress can also be elements the judge or jury will consider in assessing the award the employee will recover in the suit. Going a step further, the employee may be able to prove that physical ailments have resulted from the mental and emotional suffering caused by the retaliatory discharge. In practice, the ills suffered by the employee as a result of retaliatory discharge may run into a whole chain of untoward circumstances set in motion by the employee's illegal termination. There could be a degree of permanent physical or psychiatric impairment or vocational disability brought about by the employer's wrongful conduct.

It is also possible that the employer who has committed retaliatory discharge will have to pay punitive damages. Punitive damages are not always awarded, but when they are they can be many times the purely compensatory component of the disaffected employee's total award. Punitive damages are sums assessed as damages in private civil court suits, above and beyond the actual damages the individual person bringing the suit can establish, to punish the employer for socially unacceptable conduct and to deter that employer and other employers from ever doing the same sort of thing again. Knowing that punitive damages are potentially a factor in litigation should deter employers from conduct for which the law allows these damages to be awarded.

The courts sometimes include the disaffected employee's attorney fees in the damages to be paid by the employer. This is meant to prevent the award to the wrongfully discharged worker from being diminished by the need to pay a large contingent fee or hourly billing to the attorney or firm of attorneys who have successfully litigated the case. Whether or not they serve this purpose, awards of attorney fees represent an added incentive to the employer not to end up on the wrong end of a retaliatory discharge case.

Without further belaboring the potentially devastating consequences of retaliatory discharge, it should be apparent that business owners, executives, managers, supervisors, and human resources professionals must arrive at an understanding of how the law operates in this area. Employers must be prepared to implement policies and procedures to insure that retaliatory discharge has no part in any aspect of personnel administration.

Individual executives, managers, and supervisors within the organization should realize that their employers' liability for their actions toward their subordinates does not, as is widely and incorrectly believed, relieve them of personal legal responsibility for their own actions. This is true whether they are owners, corporate officers, directors of the business, or merely employees themselves. Although, as a matter of trial strategy, the attorneys representing a disaffected worker may choose to name only the company rather than the individual boss responsible for what has been done, there is nothing preventing suit against the boss personally for what the boss has done or allowed to take place.

Cases Defining Retaliatory Discharge

The earliest cases which recognized and defined the law of retaliatory discharge involved employees who were terminated for having filed industrial insurance claims against their employers. Industrial insurance is another term for worker's compensation. It is in force in one form or another in every state. It awards compensation to workers, regardless of fault, for lost wages, medical expenses, and in certain cases for permanent, partial, and total disability as the result of on-the-job injuries and occupational diseases.

The courts recognized that the rights workers were meant to enjoy under the worker's compensation system would be prejudiced significantly if employers were permitted to deter their employees from filing claims by being allowed to treat their employees in all circumstances as common law employees at will. That is, discharging employees who file claims, as the rule of common law employment at will ostensibly states, is the employer's unlimited prerogative but is not allowed when the employer's actual motive is coercion or retaliation for the employee's industrial insurance claim.

Employees who can prove that they have lost their jobs because they filed or intended to file for worker's compensation can sue their employers for wrongful discharge. Proof that discharge has taken place because of an actual or pending industrial insurance claim will result in the court awarding damages for the employee's loss in having his or her employment taken away.

The earliest cases in this genre recognized the purpose of the suit was two-fold. The suit makes the worker whole by replacing what the worker has lost by being fired in retaliation for exercising a legally protected right. More importantly, as a matter of social policy, the courts have dictated that employees' legal rights are protected from violation by employers' exercise of employers' usual prerogative, under the employment at-will system, to discharge employees at employers' discretion.

Employer retaliation for workers' filing compensation claims is covered here as one example, but more importantly because this specific type of case was important in the historical development of retaliatory discharge law. This one area is important in understanding the law of retaliatory discharge because it represented the basic paradigm of retaliatory discharge which the courts have greatly expanded upon since the earliest cases were first handed down.

Actually in practice, the question of whether or not a worker injured on the job must be given his or her job back, especially if the worker has sustained some sort of disability which makes full reinstatement less than feasible, is a very complex subject under state law. One needs special technical familiarity with the individual state's worker's compensation statute and regulations, which is beyond the scope of this book, to fully answer actual questions which will arise in this area. Questions surrounding reinstatement of workers after off-the-job injuries brings the law of disability discrimination into play, and this is treated in Chapter 11 of this book.

Interpretation of the Courts

The courts have expanded the law of retaliatory discharge to all sorts of situations where the employee is dismissed, or constructively dismissed, for exercising a protected legal right. The cases all have the same common denominator. The employer cannot use the usual prerogative under the doctrine of employment at will to discharge any employee, at any time, for any reason the employer sees fit, if the motivation is retaliation, coercion, or deterrence against employees' full exercise of recognized legal rights.

A substantive definition for the rights for which the employee is protected from retaliatory employer conduct is difficult to ascertain. Pieces of this definition can be garnered from individual court precedents, and then hopefully welded into a coherent whole.

Court precedents in each local jurisdiction will have controlling authority over the future decisions of its courts. Precedents handed down in other jurisdictions, although not required to be followed, may be sufficiently attractive to persuade the local courts to follow them, nonetheless.

Of course, many legal rules which are now followed by the courts were at some point in time announced in ground-breaking new decisions which were not based on prior precedents. The possibility of new legal developments represents a significant difficulty for employers and their legal counsel who sometimes have to try to base their strategic decisions on the shifting sands of judicial opinion. The ever-changing, evolutionary nature of the law does not always provide a working set of hard and fast rules most pragmatic business managers would like to have to guide them. Our common law system of jurisprudence may be disconcertingly alien to those with engineering and accounting backgrounds who are accustomed to operating in more concrete conceptual frameworks.

It is perhaps more important to look for enduring patterns in the reported judicial decisions, rather than for minutely detailed laundry lists of specific actions which have and have not been sanctioned. This is the approach which will be taken in this book.

The worker's compensation/retaliation cases are an example of a principle widely followed in this area of the law. Citizens have certain rights in our society which employers are not allowed to suppress by exercising their prerogatives as employers at will to hire and fire them at their discretion.

Any time the law allows an employee to file a complaint with a governmental agency concerning the employer's conduct, the employee cannot be made the object of retaliation for threatening or actually filing such a complaint. This includes complaints of discrimination, harassment, occupational safety and health violations, wage-and-hour violations, child labor law infractions, unlawful immigration policies, and the like. It does not matter whether the employee is complaining on his or her own behalf, or on behalf of another individual or group of individuals affected or reasonably believed to be affected by unlawful employer conduct.

Federal antidiscrimination laws and most states' antidiscrimination laws define discrimination not only to include actual discriminatory conduct toward employees, but also to include, under the rubric of illegal discrimination, retaliation or reprisals of any form for complaining about discriminatory conduct. The remedies available for discrimination, discussed in this book in the chapters on various forms of discrimination, are available as well to those who suffer untoward consequences for complaining about discrimination, whether or not they or others are actual victims of discrimination itself.

Furthermore, those who assist public agencies in investigating and prosecuting actual or alleged acts of discrimination or other unlawful conduct by employers, or those who similarly assist attorneys or parties involved in private civil court suits involving these matters, are likewise exempt from retribution or coercion by the employer. Without this protection, the rights afforded to workers under antidiscrimination, safety, wage-and-hours laws, and similar social enactments, would suffer if employers were unfairly permitted to influence the outcomes of enforcement proceedings by exerting impermissible forms of influence over the parties and witnesses.

Also related, conceptually, are complaints to public agencies over employer actions which do not specifically hinge on the relationship between employer and employee. These are similarly protected from employer retaliation. For example, an employee of a property management firm might report an employer to the authorities for discriminatory rental policies or for building code discrepancies in rental apartments. Although the employee is not a rental tenant, and the tenants are not employees, the employee making the complaint would be protected from retaliation within the context of his or her employment, in order to foster compliance with the applicable laws being violated by the employer.

Complaints by employees to the news media over their employers' policies and actions are finding protection in the courts from retaliatory employer conduct as well. One of our most fundamental rights is freedom of expression. It is based on a basic assumption that society is best served by open expression of all viewpoints, even those which are unpopular, controversial and even offensive.

The "whistle-blowing" cases are easy to understand on this basis. "Whistle-blowing" occurs when an employee is discharged or constructively discharged for public disclosure of employer conduct which is or should become a matter of public concern. Examples of cases include employees who publicize price gouging and inferior product specifications on government or defense contract work, employees who publicize questionable securities transactions or shady financial dealings by their employers, and employees who inform the media of harmful employer environmental practices or policies which are illegal or at least very damaging from a public relations standpoint.

The list of conduct for which "whistle-blowers" are protected from employer reprisal is seemingly endless. If the public has a right to know about something, the employee has the right to make it known. The employer can get into a great deal of trouble by attempting to suppress the employee's exercise of free expression in these areas.

Courts are so protective of employees' rights of free expression, where matters of public interest are potentially at stake, that a private employer can be hit with a damage suit even for retaliation against an employee who takes these matters up within proper channels inside the organization, and does not go public with potentially damaging information. The principle is the same if an employee does not follow channels implicitly, but goes over a supervisor's or manager's head with something he or she feels the immediate higher-up will not want to hear or act upon. Where the public interest is at stake, or potentially at stake, employees cannot be punished for voicing unpopular causes or bringing to light embarrassing information.

Retaliation can also occur in other very innocuous and seemingly mundane circumstances, such as adverse action against an employee who needs time off to vote on election day, or who must be absent to serve on jury duty or in the military reserves. Employees engaging in these activities are protected by law, and employers must make reasonable accommodation to their employee's rights in these areas.

Retaliatory discharge refers to loss of an employee's job for participating in legally-protected conduct. However, actual discharge is not always what occurs. Many employees have been successful in litigation over what is termed "constructive" discharge, where the parameters of their job have been altered so significantly that the court can later rule that discharge has effectively taken place.

For example, a whistle-blower might see his or her job responsibilities drastically reduced or altered, either as a form of retaliation for going public, or in an attempt to deny the individual access to additional insights into company operations which could serve as the basis of future media disclosures. If the employer's action is seen by the courts as reasonable grounds for the individual to make the decision to quit, the action of the employer could serve the same purposes as actually dismissing the individual. Under these circumstances, the decision to leave would not be treated as a voluntary resignation, but as an involuntary termination.

However, the courts have not looked favorably upon individuals who resign in protest over actions of their employers, with which they do not agree, or which they feel are illegal, immoral, or otherwise reprehensible in light of the individual's social or political outlook. Unless there is some overt action by the employer directed against the individual for the individual's own actions, convictions or opinions, the case will not be treated as one of actual or constructive retaliatory discharge for which the individual is eligible for an award of damages in court.

Unless there is an employment contract stipulating otherwise, an individual is free to resign in protest over the employer's policies or actual conduct. But without something being directed by the employer against the individual that affects the terms and conditions of the individual's employment relationship, the courts will not "go to bat" for the individual by forcing the employer in effect to change for the individual's benefit.

What Can Employers Do to Protect Themselves?

What are employers to do in light of the potential for substantial damage liability for retaliatory discharge? The simplest remedy is to keep in mind that under our post-Watergate standards of open public scrutiny, private employers and corporations, large and small, have to clean up their acts. Not only do companies have to clean up their acts, but they have to realize that when something wrong is done, trying to hide it or to suppress it may only compound the eventual damage which will result.

Whether or not one agrees with this is not the point. The courts will make believers out of those who disagree, and the only pragmatic approach is to recognize that employers' traditional freedom in making private employment decisions has been seriously circumscribed by the courts under the legal decisions against retaliatory discharge.

Employees are becoming increasingly knowledgeable about their rights and how to exploit the implicit threat posed by the possibility of a suit for damages to their advantage. Some employees will make a career out of complaining about things, things for which they have a legal right to complain, in an attempt to vaccinate themselves from the effects of legitimate disciplinary measures which might appear retaliatory after the fact.

This book stresses the importance of keeping detailed records of employee conduct, fairly and objectively for all employees, almost assuming that every legitimate disciplinary decision will be later questioned in court as retaliatory. Employers must evaluate employees fairly and impartially according to objective performance standards. Therefore, decisions which adversely affect particular employees who later threaten or actually bring suit can be demonstrated to rest on objective factors rather than retaliatory motives.

Conclusion

There really is no special magic formula for employers to follow in the area of retaliatory discharge. The best course of action is to become aware that the courts are quite ready to protect employees' rights from employers' retaliatory conduct. Employers have to get this message if they want to avoid substantial liability for wrongful discharge.

Chapter Three

Employee Work Records

The number of employers being sued throughout the United States over the contents of their employees' work records is increasing. These suits are usually framed under the law of defamation. Thus, it is important for business owners, executives, managers, supervisors, and human resources professionals to become familiar with the law of defamation, how it works, and how it can be applied to them with devastating effect if litigation ensues.

While many of the suits filed by employees in this context are not successful, the ability of management to prevail often depends on a thorough understanding of the law of defamation. It is also critical to implement effective human resource management policies which take advantage of special consideration employers will receive under the law when appropriate circumstances are present. These suits hinge, first of all, on careful application by the court of the strict definition of defamation to the facts of the case, and then, upon whether or not a qualified legal privilege will be available to insulate the employer from liability for damages even if defamation has technically taken place.

The court must first decide whether all of the basic elements of defamation are present. If any of the elements are missing, the case must be dismissed as legally unfounded. Assuming all of the elements of a case of defamation have been proven to have occurred, the defendant can still escape liability by proving that its conduct has been confined strictly within the protected realm of a recognized legal privilege. Unfortunately, however, this is not the end, because the disaffected employee can still rebut the showing of legal privilege on the employer's part by demonstrating that the employer has abused the privilege for an impermissible purpose. This shifts things around again and places the employee in a position to recover an award of damages from the court.

Law of Defamation Defined

Although the law of defamation is very technical, it is important for management to take the time and to make the effort to understand it, and to bear along with what might seem to be a tedious discussion of abstract legal principles. This task is simplified somewhat by the fact that the law of defamation is rather uniform throughout the United States, because most states have adopted the same rules from the English common law. In addition, there are certain constitutional considerations of free speech involved which are matters of uniform national judicial policy.

Defamation is a term which encompasses both libel and slander. Libel is written defamation; slander refers to purely oral communication of a defamatory nature. Libel, as opposed to slander, was considered under the eighteenth-century English common law to be a more serious affair than slander, and there were very different rules for proving and assessing damages depending on whether libel or slander had taken place.

The distinction between libel and slander has lost its significance in modern court precedents. The law now concerns itself with whether defamation has occurred and the consequences to the disaffected party if it has. It is not particularly bothered by the largely archaic distinctions between libel and slander. Libel, slander, and defamation are now used more or less interchangeably, despite the fact that traditionally each had its own separate meaning.

Defamation occurs when a derogatory statement is communicated about a certain person, which lowers or tends to lower the person's standing in the opinions of others. It is necessary that the statement actually pertain directly to the person bringing the suit and that the statement be derogatory. These two elements are essential under the textbook definition of defamation, but they are usually so obvious one way or the other in most practical contexts that they do not need to be belabored further.

The most important element of defamation is that the derogatory statement must be communicated to someone other than the person making the statement or the person to whom the statement refers. This means that placing something uncomplimentary in an employee's personnel file is not, in and of itself, defamatory. Nor is it defamatory to tell an employee that his or her abilities, performance, or attitude are faulty or less than desirable.

Circulating employment information or evaluations among persons within the organization is also not considered defamatory, regardless of what the information is or what the file may contain. For defamation to occur, the law requires "publication" of the allegedly defamatory material. Keeping the information within the file and circulating personnel information, or discussing the employee only within proper channels inside the organization, simply will not serve as the basis for a successful defamation suit.

It is as if the law views the organization as one entity, essentially talking to itself, when information is recorded and kept in its files, is circulated strictly within accepted channels, and is not publicized to unauthorized individuals who have no reason to know, and is not disseminated outside the organization. There have been cases where the party bringing the suit has lost sight of this elementary requirement, and these cases resulted in dismissal in favor of the employer on the basis that no "publication" in the legal sense has taken place.

How the Law of Defamation Works

The successfully litigated cases of defamation involving employee work records have all involved dissemination of derogatory information about the employee outside of the organization, almost always to another prospective employer. The disaffected employee typically claims that his or her career advancement and chances of continued employment within a particular field depend on favorable, or at least fair and impartial, references being given to prospective employers concerning his or her abilities, attitude, and job performance.

Of course, the fact that unfavorable information is in an employee's or former employee's file may be just an accident looking for a place to happen, as it may be inevitable at some point that this information will get out. However, until it actually gets out there is technically no basis for a lawsuit.

The lurking potential for litigation liability is especially acute when an employee has been dismissed, asked to resign or, in effect, forced out by being passed over for expected promotions or salary increases. Or, an employee may have chosen voluntarily to quit, but while still with the company may have been evaluated less positively or promoted less rapidly than what the employee would consider indicative of his or her true capabilities. Employees in these circumstances, (more likely in the case of dismissal or forced resignation) might sue claiming that the dismissal or absence of favorable advancement itself was an act of defamation, whose consequences, such as diminished future earning potential, are the employer's legal responsibility.

The fact of dismissal, forced resignation, or less rapid advancement than desired, in and of itself, is usually not considered grounds for a defamation suit, even though conceivably any such course of action implies the existence of opinions about the employee, which, if and when communicated to a prospective employer, could constitute defamation. Communicating the grounds for dismissal to a prospective employer could conceivably amount to defamation, if the employer is not protected by legal privilege or another more direct strategy designed to avert possible liability.

Strategies to Avoid Legal Liability

One potential strategy, which employers surprisingly often do not think of using, is to require a written authorization and waiver of liability before any information whatsoever will be released on behalf of a former employee or existing employee who is looking around for another job. This should be required before anyone will talk about the employee or acknowledge that he or she was ever employed. In fact many states have strict statutes which forbid unauthorized release of employment records.

The court might be able to infer from the fact that an employee has listed the employer on a resume or job application that the employee has authorized the employer to release information about the employee, but this is not necessarily always the case. Where potential legal liability is at stake it usually pays to err, if at all, only on the side of extra caution and get a signed release from the employee.

Some states have statutes which allow employees and former employees the right of access to their personal files for a certain period of time after cessation of employment. These statutes, where they are in effect, also typically require employers to consider challenges to the truth and sufficiency of the information contained in the employee's or former employee's file, as well as to place a record of the employee's challenge in the file and the employer's response.

The whole point of such a challenge is the prospect that matters from the file will later be released to prospective employers. Thus, even when there is no such statute in effect in the local jurisdiction, employers should take it seriously when an employee demands to see his or her personnel file and voices a challenge to what it contains. The employer might be able to head off a much more serious confrontation later on by taking the time to get a written statement from the employee of objections to what has or has not gained entry into the records. The employer should also consider carefully what the employee has to say and make a written record in the file of how the matter was decided and how the decision was communicated to the employee.

The strategy employers have most widely used in litigation over employee work records is reliance on one or more legal privileges the law affords them when handling releases of information from employees' files. A legal privilege, in very general terms, is special permission to do something, under special circumstances, which would be illegal where the circumstances giving rise to the privilege are not present.

Most of the litigation over defamation in the context of employee personnel records, if it is not dismissed because the element of publication is lacking, centers on whether the employer has a legal privilege to disseminate information as it has, and whether the employer has gone outside the bounds of what is protected under the privilege if it is available. Once in court, however, it is too late to change the facts. It is necessary for employers to structure their affairs in this context before the fact, in order to be able to take full advantage of legal privileges the law affords to them.

Judges and lawyers learn in law school that truth offers a privilege and is a defense to defamation charges. Truth is an absolute defense to defamation, in cases where celebrities and public figures sue the media. However, when private individuals are involved, whose fitness for their jobs is not a matter of public concern, truth is only a defense if the person responsible for communicating derogatory matters to others can prove there is some good reason for letting those others in on what has been communicated.

Truth is a privilege, but only to the extent that private parties have a good, legally accepted reason for giving out information from an employee's file or for discussing the employee's work history, job record, or qualifications with a party outside of the organization where the information originated.

The law has established that prospective employers have a legitimate interest in assessing the fitness of prospective employees, which will justify former and existing employers in disseminating information to each other to make such assessments. When releasing information for this limited purpose, employers have a legal privilege to disseminate derogatory information, as long as the information is true.

The privilege is available only as long as it is used to convey fair and objective information to prospective employers, who have asked for such information, to allow them to make the decision whether or not to hire the individual in question. Any time the privilege which ostensibly exists in this context is used out of spite, or "malice" as the law terms it, to hurt someone or to damage their

Chapter Four

Employee Noncompetition Agreements

Noncompetition agreements with employees are an important part of personnel management strategy in businesses where employees who might leave to become competitors are perceived as an acute threat to the business' continued existence and economic vitality. These agreements, however, have often run into serious problems of enforcement in court. Management must address these problems before getting to court.

It is important to distinguish noncompetition agreements with employees from noncompetition agreements that typically accompany purchases and sales of businesses and professional practices. While the former often entail problems of judicial enforcement which must be addressed when these agreements are only in the strategic planning phase, the latter are generally enforced in court without much difficulty.

The law sees it as fundamental to the sale of a business or professional practice that the seller must refrain from carrying on competing business or professional activities within a certain geographic and temporal framework after the sale. This gives meaning to the very idea that the seller's business has been sold to the buyer and

31

that the seller is actually giving up something which the buyer receives in the bargain.

Noncompetition agreements between sellers and buyers of existing businesses or professional practices are not within the scope of this book. It must be kept in mind that the principles discussed here apply only to the special case of noncompetition agreements between employers and their employees.

Similarly, this book does not deal with overt noncompetition agreements between existing businesses. Federal and state antitrust laws are likely to deem such agreements completely illegal.

This discussion assumes throughout that the party described as the "employee" is actually a *former* employee not still actively employed by the employer hurt by his or her competing activities when the competing activities under consideration take place. Noncompetition agreements with former employees are subject to strict legalities and are more often honored in the breach than in the observance. However, a state of noncompetition between an employee and his or her existing employer is virtually taken for granted, unless there is a specific term in the employment relationship which would permit such conduct to take place during the existence of the employment relationship.

Employment is a confidential relationship which the law assumes the employee will not exploit to an existing employer's detriment. An employee owes the employer undivided loyalty, but only until the relationship is terminated by one side or the other. Then the rules governing the employer and former employee change markedly, if there are any actual rules left at that point.

Employee noncompetition agreements are meant to address the fact that many business enterprises are quite vulnerable to the effects of competition from employees who leave to go to work for competing concerns or to set up their own shops. The law is willing to give certain employers some measure of relief if they are willing to abide by the rules governing employee noncompetition agreements and to stay within the limitations which the law has placed upon them in this context.

Some businesses are vulnerable because they have special assets for which the owners want special protection. Assets are not only the tangible physical property, real estate, inventory, and bank deposits which show up on financial statements, but they include intangibles like production, distribution, pricing, and marketing strategies. Those intangibles have been developed with formidable investments of time, effort, expense, and trusting relationships with established clients and customers, all of which generally were acquired with considerable difficulty.

Intangible Assets

Employees obviously are prohibited from expropriating their employers' furniture, machinery, and cash by the simple fact that there are laws against robbery, theft, and embezzlement. The same is true of office books, files, lists, Rolodexes, and computer disks. But with intangible assets the rules are not so simple. The criminal laws, with only certain exceptions, do not prevent employees from taking away a significant amount of information. This includes what they have in their heads when they clean out their desks and walk out of the office for the last time or other information which they may have carefully placed in files of their own or can reconstruct from public sources.

Many times businesses will have products or processes which are not sufficiently unique or different from prior art to be patented, or advertising concepts which do not involve a recognized trademark, or which cannot be copyrighted. Or the only thing they may have developed are rather ephemeral relationships with clients and customers. The only hope for protection of these potentially valuable assets might be employee noncompetition agreements with key individuals in the organization.

Patents

Employers who have patents covering their products or production methods are protected during the life of the patent from an employee, or anyone else for that matter, who infringes on the patent by developing and marketing a product or using a production technique so similar that patent infringement takes place. But the rules of patent law require that the subject of a patent strictly meet the legal criteria of novelty and usefulness before a patent can be granted. If a patent is not or cannot be granted, a valuable but easily duplicated product or process may be fair game for anyone, including former employees not covered by a noncompetition agreement.

Trademarks

Trademarks which are properly registered under state and federal law are another source of protection from competition. But there may always be someone who will come along with a very similar mark or product name, different enough to get by the strict provisions of trademark law, who can compete unfairly, albeit legally, with the original trademark owner.

Copyright

Copyright is a means of obtaining legal protection for an original work of authorship as it is expressed in a tangible medium of expression. Books, promotional literature, and advertising copy can be protected from unauthorized duplication and use, but underlying ideas, concepts, methods, and thought processes used to formulate or embodied into copyrighted works are not themselves the property of the copyright holder. The copyrighted book, ad, TV spot, or slogan *itself* is protected from unauthorized copying and use.

Departing Employees

The threat posed to the employer's intangible business assets by departing employees is very real. Often the factors which make employees who move laterally within a particular industry most attractive to new employers are their knowledge of their former employers' successful methods or, more likely, their personal relationships with key individuals in various capacities within the industry with whom the new employer would like to develop working relationships.

In personal service businesses and many professions, prospective new employees are often evaluated solely on the basis of their ability to attract new business to their new employers, which is a polite way of asking whether or not they will be able to bring their old employers' customers or clients with them when they change jobs.

New businesses have a poor track record, and only a small fraction of those started each year actually survive after depletion of their original working capital. Those new businesses which actually make it are often those where employees have left a particular employer and have taken customers and clients, or proven distribution, pricing, and marketing methods with them from their old employers.

Organizations should consider entering into noncompetition agreements with a number of employees. Some of these include: employees in strategic positions within the organization, particularly those in sales or marketing; employees who have developed personal bonds of loyalty to the firm's customers and clients; and employees in executive positions who would be able to set up competing businesses modeled along the lines of their former employer.

Policy of the Law

As much as businesses need noncompetition agreements with certain employees, the law looks upon these agreements with disdain. The social policies and laws of this country are meant to embody a strong tradition of aversion toward restraint of unlimited economic opportunity and freedom of competition. The antitrust laws prevent almost every species of overt restraint on competition by noncompetitive agreements between businesses. When businesses are dealing with their individual employees, the law finds it necessary to protect to a great extent the right of each person to earn his or her livelihood in a chosen profession or line of work, free from contractual restraint, even where that means going directly into competition with a former employer. On the other hand, certain businesses are seen as peculiarly vulnerable to employees exploiting their relationships with their employers unfairly to their own advantage. The law will allow and enforce employee noncompetition agreements in these instances, but only as long as they are kept within accepted bounds and used only to protect the employers' recognized legitimate interests.

In most commercial contractual settings, the policy of the law is that agreements are made to be kept. The party who is not in compliance with any garden-variety commercial contract must prove in court that there are exceptional circumstances justifying noncompliance, or run up against the power of the court to enforce the contract by issuing injunctions prohibiting noncompliance and/or awarding damages to compensate the other party for its losses.

Drafting, Negotiating and Enforcing

The most important lesson for business management in drafting, negotiating, and trying to enforce employee noncompetition agreements is that the customary rules of contract law are turned about one-hundred-eighty degrees where employee noncompetition agreements are concerned. The law almost assumes that these agreements are not valid, that they only represent attempts by employers to overstep the bounds of legal propriety and to prejudice unfairly the inalienable right of every citizen to earn a living in the business of profession of his or her choice after leaving a particular employer's employment.

When going to court to enforce an employee noncompetition agreement, the employer must show that unusual circumstances exist to justify enforcement of the agreement. Otherwise, the agreement will be thrown out, and the employer will be left with nothing in the way of legal protection. It will not matter that the employee freely admits signing the agreement and that it ostensibly prevents conduct the employee is then engaged in. If the employer cannot show the agreement falls into the narrow range of circumstances under which employee noncompetition agreements may be enforced, the agreement will be void.

The first consideration in drafting and negotiating such an agreement, and planning personnel and management strategy around whether or not such an agreement will be successful, is to recognize that some states have specific statutes on the subject of noncompetition agreements with employees. Although knowledgeable local legal counsel would presumably be brought in anyway whenever any important legal matter is under consideration, it is essential that counsel make sure that local law on the subject of employee noncompetition agreements is consulted and observed scrupulously to the letter.

Even in the absence of an explicit statute, many states have detailed case precedents which define the parameters under which employee noncompetition agreements can be used and will be enforced. Some states may have gone so far as to have specific precedents outlining the rules for specific businesses and professional callings.

Geographic and Time Restrictions

State law typically will impose geographic and time restrictions on noncompetition agreements with employees and may indicate specifically which businesses and professions can use them and which cannot. Obviously, state law on this subject must be followed to a tee.

It is important to realize how the courts handle the specific limitations on the geographic and temporal scope of noncompetition agreements when these agreements later come to the courts for interpretation and enforcement. Any attempt to exceed the geographic and temporal limits imposed by state law will render the agreement completely void. If the agreement is void, the court will not go back and rewrite the agreement to include enforceable terms in place of terms which are too expansive to be enforced; the court will simply throw it out.

For example, if state law says that a noncompetition agreement can cover a route salesperson in the county where he or she worked for a period of one year, no more than those parameters can be written into a noncompetition agreement. If the agreement covers more than that county, or goes beyond one year, the agreement will be void, period. The court will not enforce the agreement only in the one county or only for one year, as it could have done if the agreement had been so drafted; the court will simply dismiss with prejudice the suit to enforce the agreement and the former employee will be left free to compete with the former employer, at any time, anywhere, by any otherwise legal means.

Even where there are no restrictions on geographic and temporal scope of employee noncompetition agreements specifically mandated by state law, the employer is wise to tone down its demands over these issues. If the court later determines, on nothing more than general principles of fairness to the employee, that an employee noncompetition agreement is too expansive or unduly burdens the employee's continued ability to earn a livelihood, the court is likely to throw out the whole agreement and not enforce what it thinks would have been a fair arrangement between the employer and former employee.

Whenever geographic and time restrictions are written into a noncompetition agreement, they must be spelled out clearly. Ambiguities which lead to difficulties of interpretation will always be resolved against the employer.

Geographic limitations must be spelled out explicitly in terms of states, counties, cities and perhaps even specific blocks within a city or a specific number of feet radius away from a certain landmark such as the former employer's office or store. Something like, "wherever the employer shall have an established retail presence" or "within the relevant market zone" are much too vague and will not suffice.

Similarly, time must be spelled out with specific dates, even though this means that once the specified expiration date has passed there is clearly nothing left for the employer to do but live with the new competitive situation. "So long as the employer shall enjoy a significant market share" or "until the employer shall have attained" a specified sales objective will not do, and any agreement containing anything like this will go right out the courthouse window if it is ever brought before a judge for enforcement.

The Employer's Existing Legitimate Interests at the Time of Termination

Keeping the breadth of specified geographic and temporal limits on postemployment competitive activities within accepted bounds is

Chapter Five

Organizational Risk Management

Risk management refers to the process by which the organization takes stock of its actual and potential legal liabilities and devises strategies to combat them. Liabilities in this context can mean suits by employees over employment-related issues such as discrimination and wrongful discharge. Liabilities can also include suits against the organization and individuals within the organization for negligent and intentional wrongful conduct for which the organization will be financially responsible.

Employment-related legal liability can also occur when claims or actual lawsuits are advanced against the organization for things which employees do to outside parties. This can also include claims or lawsuits from outside parties as a result of actions and omissions by persons within the organization for whom the organization is financially responsible.

Somewhere in between both situations are cases of on-the-job injury, where the person who suffers loss due to injury is a member of the organizational community who may have been wronged by the employer's conduct or that of a coworker. It is important to be able to recognize worker's compensation claims as worker's compensation claims, because these claims generally represent a lower level of compensation than civil court suits. In addition, the worker's compensation system strictly limits the circumstances in which injured workers are able to bring civil suits against their employers.

Legal Responsibility of Business Enterprises

As a general proposition, business enterprises can exist as sole proprietorships, partnerships, or corporations. The starting point is to realize that the business enterprise, in whatever legal form it has adopted, is legally liable for wrongful conduct of its employees, if that conduct was undertaken within the course and scope of the employment duties of the employee who commits the wrongful act.

Sole Proprietorship

A sole proprietorship is an individual doing business in his or her own name without the benefit of corporate status. The owner is personally liable for everything that takes place, including actions of employees within the course and scope of their employment. All of the owner's assets are on the line to satisfy any liability judgment handed down by a court, with certain exemptions provided by state and federal laws on the subjects of homestead, debtors' rights and bankruptcy, which are too complicated to explore here.

Partnership

A partnership exists when one or more individuals operate a business together under an explicit or implicit understanding that they will share management responsibilities and the financial risks and rewards of the enterprise. A formal partnership agreement is not necessary. Many states have adopted the Uniform Partnership Act, or have other legal criteria for deciding whether individuals in business together are in fact operating as a partnership. This becomes important when an adverse court judgment is made and it is necessary to apportion financial responsibility for the enterprise's obligations.

Partners, and all of their personal assets not exempted under state and federal homestead, bankruptcy, and debtor/creditor law, are on the line for the obligations of the partnership. The obligations of the partnership include all debts incurred by the partnership or by any of its individual members acting for the partnership, and liability for all wrongful acts of individual partners acting for the partnership and employees acting within the course and scope of their employment by the partnership.

Corporations

Corporations are considered separate legal entities apart from the individuals who form them, run them, and invest in them. Corporations only exist when and as long as they are recognized and authorized to transact business by the corporations division of the state where they are chartered. Corporations must do business under the name and according to the articles of incorporation and bylaws drawn up by the incorporators and placed on file with the state.

The corporation is liable for all debts undertaken by officers and employees who have authority to enter into debts on behalf of the corporation. Individuals who incur debts for the corporation are not personally liable for these debts, unless the creditor, as creditors often do, requires them to undertake separate personal liability as additional security for payment of the debt by the corporation.

The corporation is also liable for all wrongful conduct of officers and employees which is performed within the course and scope of their recognized duties on behalf of the corporation. Officers, directors, and employees are not personally liable for the wrongful conduct of other persons which is nevertheless attributable to the corporation.

Stockholders, who may or may not also be officers, directors, or employees, are financially responsible as stockholders only to the extent that they can lose the benefit of the funds or other assets they have invested in the corporation by purchasing its stock. Due to excessive legal obligations or other factors, the corporation may be unable to pay dividends or may go out of business with the stock investment depreciated in value or actually valueless, but that is the extent of the risk faced by a stockholder in a corporation.

Limited Partnerships

Limited partnerships are somewhere in between ordinary partnerships and corporations. The general partners have the same status as partners in ordinary partnerships, while the limited partners, who take no active hand in running the business and are involved only as passive investors, are treated like corporate stockholders. Limited partnerships always require a written limited partnership agreement to be filed with state and/or local authorities.

Legal Liability of Employees While Performing Duties for the Corporation

This discussion leads up to one of the most commonly misunderstood aspects of vicarious liability and financial responsibility in the corporate context. Most people wrongly believe that because an individual works for a corporation or is an officer or director of a corporation, the individual is immune from legal liability for his or her own wrongful conduct which is performed within the course and scope of his or her duties for the corporation. This is just not the case. Everyone is personally legally responsible for the consequences of his or her own wrongful actions. There simply is no defense of superior orders in the context of corporate enterprise. Persons are not responsible for the independent actions of other persons within the corporation, as they would be for the actions of their partners. And persons are not personally responsible for debts of the corporation which they have taken out on behalf of the corporation, assuming the creditor consents to the debt being treated as a purely corporate obligation. But they remain fully accountable for their own legally impermissible or wrongful conduct.

In determining the nature and consequences of legal liability in this context, the law makes a distinction between negligent conduct and intentional conduct.

Negligent Conduct

Negligence consists in causing personal injury or property damage by doing what a reasonably careful person would not do under the circumstances, or failing to do what a reasonably careful person would. Most common garden-variety personal injury suits, like motor vehicle accidents and premises liability cases, involve allegations of negligence. Negligence might arise from failing to use due care and caution while driving a business vehicle or failing to keep retail business premises up to accepted maintenance standards and causing a customer to fall down and get hurt.

A court, in general, is more likely to find negligence to fall within the course and scope of an employee's duties than intentional injurious misconduct. The employee being authorized or directed to perform certain tasks like driving or mopping the floor carries with it the implicit understanding that the employee will be guilty of lapses of attention which will result in unintended consequences.

An employer who directs an employee to drive a vehicle assumes responsibility for accidents the employee encounters in the normal course of his or her duties as a driver. Cases arise where drivers use company vehicles on company time to run personal errands or goof off when accidents occur. The argument is that these accidents are not within the course and scope of employment, and the employer is not responsible.

The courts usually bend over backward to find some way of compensating the victim of an employee's negligence at the employer's expense. For example, the court might hold that slight digressions from duty are still within the course and scope of employment, while only major derelictions, such as going on a drunken bender and driving a company vehicle cross-country to Las Vegas or Atlantic City are not. Risk managers should assume that the company will be liable for the negligence of an employee entrusted with a company vehicle, up to the point where the employee commits a criminal misappropriation of the company's property by misuse of the vehicle.

Most states hold the owner of a vehicle responsible for the driver's actions, unless the vehicle is actually considered stolen, which may render it unnecessary for the court to consider the parameters of the course and scope of employment to render a decision adverse to the employer.

Intentional Conduct

On the other hand, most intentional wrongdoing will be seen by the courts to fall outside the scope of the average employee's duties. Cases of intentional wrongdoing usually involve assaults on other persons or theft of their property. But some occupations may represent exceptions to the general rule of nonliability, such as security personnel or those who perform repossessions on behalf of creditors, where the intentional use of force against persons or property is an expected part of the job.

There is an important loophole in the general rule of employer nonliability for intentional wrongdoing by employees. This loophole exists where the victim successfully alleges negligence by the employer in the selection and training of employees, which should have been undertaken by the employer to prevent the occurrence of intentional misconduct. Examples of this may include theft or violence, or in failing to institute other safeguards to identify, correct, and weed-out individual employees who are likely to commit intentional wrongs affecting the security and well-being of clients or the public at large.

Attorneys, accountants, financial planners, real estate agents, and certain paraprofessional employees of professional firms are in special positions where intentional misconduct may occur. They may be able to profit financially from the relationship of trust between their employers and their clients, should they choose to commit fraud or embezzlement at the expense of their clients. Security guard companies, private firms which employ security personnel, restaurants and bars which employ bouncers and doormen, even day care centers, group homes, and nursing homes which cater to vulnerable and infirm clients, are acutely vulnerable to suits from persons intentionally assaulted and abused by their employees.

Insurance Coverage

The most practical consequence of the distinction between negligent and intentional wrongdoing has to do with insurance coverage. No U.S. jurisdiction permits insurance coverage to be issued for intentional wrongful conduct, while insurance is available for nearly every conceivable form of negligence. Employers are able to insure themselves for ordinary negligence, such as what happens in garden-variety vehicle accidents and accidental injuries on commercial premises. They also can insure themselves for negligence in failing to select, train, supervise, audit, discipline, and terminate their employees in a manner calculated to see that they do not perpetrate intentional wrongs of their own, which are intentional from the standpoint of the actual individual committing them, but only negligence in terms of the employer's responsibility.

Another important consideration is that federal bankruptcy law permits a debtor to discharge, that is, completely wipe clean, its liability for negligence, whether or not that liability is founded on a court judgment, a pending court action, or merely exists as the possibility that suit seeking judgment will eventually be filed. Liability for intentional wrongful conduct cannot be discharged in bankruptcy proceedings. Again, bankruptcy and debtor/creditor law is too complicated to discuss in more detail than this.

As a practical matter, most employers, corporate or individual, do not have appreciable assets lying around waiting for injured parties to sue them for. What physical assets they have are usually committed to some essential purpose, and liquid assets are dedicated to payroll, tax, or short-term debt liability, or are disbursed to the shareholders as dividends. Any substantial run on the corporation's assets, to respond to a civil personal injury or damages suit, will force the enterprise into bankruptcy, which in turn will put a hold on all claims against the employer and possibly result in discharge of the claim which gave rise to the suit.

Thus, the employer's insurance coverage is what nearly every personal injury or property damage suit seeks. Many of the best negligence attorneys will not take a case, no matter how healthy the corporate defendant may appear, unless there is insurance available to pay the claim if it is successful.

Getting appropriate and adequate liability insurance coverage is thus an essential part, perhaps even the only means, many companies will take to meet their needs in the risk-management context. Liability insurance encompasses two basic obligations by the insurance carrier—the duty to defend and the duty to indemnify.

The Duty to Defend

The duty to defend means that the insurer must provide a legal defense to the insured for any claim which appears to fall within the terms of the coverage which has been written. Discharge of the duty to defend by the insurance company may entail simply having an adjuster contact the claimant, conduct whatever additional investigation of the claim is appropriate, and settle with the claimant by getting a release of the claim against the insured in exchange for the agreed settlement amount. Or, the insurer may have to hire and pay for legal counsel to represent the insured in litigation, in addition to trying to keep settlement negotiations going on while the court case progresses, and paying the judgment if the case cannot be settled and proceeds to entry of judgment against the insured.

The insurer is liable for all attorney fees and litigation expenses. Some policies even reimburse the insured and its employees for loss of time while away from work participating in depositions, trial and other court proceedings or otherwise assisting defense counsel with the insured's defense.

The insurer, on the other hand, has the prerogative of selecting defense counsel for the insured and can insist that the insured cooperate with counsel in presenting the defense in the manner that counsel deems appropriate in its legal judgment. Actually this situation opens up a whole Pandora's box of ethical dilemmas for defense counsel selected by the insurance company. Counsel must represent the client, who is the insured, and may not follow the direction of its principal, the insurance company, if the insurance company's strategic objectives significantly compromise the insured's interests.

Sometimes there is a significant conflict between the interests of individual employees named as defendants in a particular suit and the interests of their employers. An individual may wish to defend himself on the basis that he or she did not do or did not have a part in what was alleged to have been done and may want to exonerate himself or herself by spilling the beans on who actually did it. The individual or the employer may want to admit responsibility and allow settlement to take place, or as a matter of trial tactics, fight to the bitter end.

In these situations the insurance company must find independent counsel for all individual parties or factions, ostensibly on the same side of the case, who have conflicting interests in the formulation of defense strategy, the conduct of the trial, or the outcome of the case. This means separate attorneys from separate law firms will appear, with their separate meters running, at all stages of the litigation. All will have the ethical obligation to go it alone or participate in the presentation of a united front, as necessary to represent their separate clients' interests.

The Duty to Indemnify

Top management, officers, and directors of corporations usually insist that their employment contracts with the corporation permit them to call upon the company for defense and indemnity of claims made against them personally. The contract will usually specify whether the company will fulfill this obligation by purchasing liability coverage for them or by some other means.

Liability insurance is sold with coverage limits defining the outer scope of the insurer's responsibility and with deductibles which set out the minimal level the insured must pay before the duty to indemnify comes into effect. The premium for insurance is lower when the deductible limit is higher. For example, most vehicle accident claims are settled for less than $10,000, and a $10,000 deductible means the insured will pay most claims on his or her own. Few claims will reach the $1,000,000 level, so dollar for dollar the first few tens of thousands of dollars of coverage are much more expensive than even million dollar increments over and above the one-million dollar level.

stolen off into the night after being sued enough times that continued viable operations are out of the question.

Legislation in many states is now limiting the rights of product liability victims, and concern over practical redress of environmental problems is in most cases now a matter of political or governmental policy outside the bounds of traditional private civil court litigation.

Worker's Compensation

Worker's compensation represents a special area of organizational risk management. Most on-the-job injuries are not compensable within the every-day rules of civil liability outlined above. Where the injury occurs within the course and scope of the employee's duties, the employee must file for compensation, if at all, within the worker's compensation, or, as it is sometimes called, industrial insurance, system and cannot sue in court.

It does not matter whether the employee was at fault for his or her own injuries, whether a coworker was at fault, whether the employer was guilty of safety violations or less than adequate concern for workers' occupational safety and health, or whether the injury was purely an accident for which no one is to blame. Worker's compensation is the exclusive remedy, as far as the employer and its employees are concerned, for on-the-job injuries.

Worker's compensation or industrial insurance provides basic time loss compensation, medical costs, certain rehabilitative expenses, and may pay an award for permanent partial or permanent total disability. Payment in the prescribed amounts is guaranteed for covered on-the-job injuries, even where there was no negligence or intentional wrongdoing by the employer or another employee to justify liability under the conventional civil rules for liability for wrongful conduct. However, the amounts awarded under the industrial insurance system are much smaller than those recovered in successful civil personal injury suits.

If the employee wants industrial insurance benefits, and is not trying to sue the employer or a coworker, the system will give the employee the benefit of the doubt in a difficult case which involves the question of whether the employee has actually suffered an injury on, as opposed to off, the job. In most cases there will be no question whether the employee was or was not on the job, but with outside sales people and executives it may not be so easy to decide when they were working and when they were not.

On the other hand, where the employee decides to sue the employer or another employee, the system says that the employer and fellow employees are immune from suit for an on-the-job injury, and the case will likely be thrown out of court.

As a practical matter most employers will have no control over how worker's compensation or industrial insurance claims are handled. There will either be a private worker's compensation carrier or an adjuster from the state-managed fund responsible for handling the claim. Participation in one or the other scheme is usually a mandatory condition for having employees at all and for carrying out day-to-day operations. The only exceptions are for large, well-established concerns who can qualify under state law as self-insurers, who employ their own claims managers and pay claims from their own assets dedicated to this purpose. The process of being self-insured and managing self-insured claims is different in each state and is too complex for the present discussion. Self-insured employers almost invariably maintain a staff of professional adjusters with previous experience within the system who manage all aspects of the claims process.

One thing to keep in mind is that worker's compensation or industrial insurance only applies to the relationship between an employer and its employees. Employees of subcontractors or employment agencies who happen to be performing work on the premises or for the employer are only barred from suing their own employers and are not barred from suing the company which is actually making use of their services, if this company is not their actual employer. If such a suit results, all of the rules of negligence and intentional wrongdoing discussed above will come into play to determine whether the company is liable.

State law generally limits the ability of all but certain designated professional employees to be defined as independent contractors to escape responsibility on the employer's part for industrial insurance premiums. Given the immunity from suit which employers enjoy with respect to their employees for on-the-job injury, it may be more sensible in the long run to treat as many individuals as possible who perform services on the premises as the company's own employees.

Stress, chronic and degenerative illness, and second-hand cigarette smoke claims present special situations where it is not clear whether worker's compensation benefits must be paid, or, more importantly, whether immunity from suit is available to the employer. These issues are developed more fully in other chapters of this book dealing more specifically with these topics.

Conclusion

There are no easy answers to questions arising in this area. Adequate liability insurance is a must for all soberly-managed enterprises. Professional claims adjusters are often necessary, and competent legal counsel often must be consulted to assess the full magnitude of the risk being encountered. Potential liabilities should never be discounted without adequate investigation.

Chapter Six

On-The-Job Stress

Claims for on-the-job stress are relatively new additions to the gamut of potential legal difficulties in store for employers from disaffected employees. The numbers of these cases are multiplying, but the results are far from universally favorable to the employees and former employees bringing these suits.

A workable understanding of the principles under which the law distinguishes meritorious from unmeritorious on-the-job stress claims is extremely useful for business owners, executives, managers, and supervisors who must make pragmatic decisions where these claims are concerned. Naturally, it is important to see what can be done to prevent these cases from arising in the first place, but preventative measures are not as easily accomplished in this area as in other areas like discrimination or wrongful discharge.

Whenever a claim for on-the-job stress arises, a decision must be made whether to ignore it, to attempt to reach settlement, or to fight the claim and take a chance that the court will vindicate the employer.

These decisions are never easy. Unmeritorious claims can be extraordinarily expensive to defend even to the point of a favorable conclusion. Attorney fees and litigation expenses of $50,000 to $100,000 would not be at all unusual to defend even a relatively simple case which goes to trial and is upheld on appeal. On the other hand, many employment law cases can be settled for less than the cost of defending them successfully. The problem, however, is that settlement with one party can open the floodgates to other similar cases on behalf of other parties expecting a relatively easy "nuisance value" settlement.

Intelligent risk-management decisions must be made on the basis of individual factors present in the specific situation under consideration. All that can be done here is to acquaint owners and personnel management with the principles at play in on-the-job stress litigation to enable them to make decisions based on a sound understanding of applicable law.

Stress is something which everyone must live with. A certain amount of it is good for us, even essential for normal physical and mental processes to function. When stress reaches pathological levels, however, it can cause a whole range of untoward physical and mental complaints. Many individuals will react by turning to the legal system for compensation of one sort or another.

Eligibility for Worker's Compensation

The first line of defense might be to regard the objective symptoms of stress as conditions for which worker's compensation or industrial insurance should pay benefits. Worker's compensation or industrial insurance, two terms used interchangeably here and elsewhere, is a system which pays benefits to workers for lost wages, medical expenses, rehabilitation costs, and permanent partial and total disability for on-the-job injuries and occupational illnesses. The system is in force in one form or another in every state in the United States.

To understand the considerations which come into play in evaluating on-the-job stress with respect to eligibility for worker's compensation, it is necessary to understand something of how the worker's compensation system operates. The system's fundamental historical and philosophical underpinnings are more important to examine than just the day-to-day details of claims management. The basic rationale behind worker's compensation was that there would be a trade-off between the certainty of payment under the system, for conditions compensable under the system, and the fact that the benefits available would be far lower than the worker would be able to recover if the worker were successful with a civil court negligence suit against the employer for personal injuries sustained on the job.

It first became apparent in the nineteenth century that modern mechanized industry and transportation could exact a terrible price from factory and railroad workers—in the form of broken bones, amputated limbs, broken bodies, and even death. Society bore a tremendous cost through the loss of productive persons due to catastrophic injury. The loss of these individual workers' ability to support their families translated into increased social welfare costs or, more likely, increased social misery among the working classes.

The civil courts were an inappropriate place for workers to seek redress, because most of the new industrial accidents, as horrible as they might have been, were not the fault of the employer. Negligence on the employer's part, as the law understands it, could rarely be proven to have caused an industrial accident to have taken place. The courts also held that fault of a fellow worker was not considered fault of the employer. The courts also tended to rule that in accepting employment in a dangerous occupation the employee had voluntarily taken the risk that injury would occur and could not sue once it eventually did. Contingent fees in injury cases are a twentieth century innovation. Even where the nineteenth-century worker could bear the legal expense and delay in getting his or her case to civil court, the worker almost always lost the case and came away without compensation.

The solution had to come through legislative action. It resulted in establishment of worker's compensation or industrial insurance systems in every state, roughly between 1890 and 1920. For accidental on-the-job injuries and occupational illnesses recognized as compensable under the system, the worker receives benefits, whether or not the employer, a fellow employee, or the employee was or was not at fault. Benefits include compensation for lost wages, medical costs, some rehabilitation expenses, and payment for permanent partial or permanent total disability.

Benefits do not include compensation for pain and suffering, mental anguish or emotional distress, loss of the ability to enjoy life, or any of the intangible factors which often inflate jury awards in civil court injury cases beyond the actual "hard" costs associated with compensating victims of accidental injury. Nor is there any compensation for lost future earnings or lost future earning capacity beyond the amounts specified by worker's compensation statutes for permanent partial or permanent total disability. The amounts are generally far lower than what would be available in civil court for these elements of damages.

For the employer, the most important factor in the worker's compensation system is that the employer cannot be sued in civil court for any injury or occupational illness which is recognized as compensable under worker's compensation. If the claim is compensable under worker's compensation, the worker cannot sue the employer, whether or not the affected worker chooses to file a worker's compensation claim, or would prefer to file suit rather than filing for worker's compensation benefits.

At this point it may be apparent what the implication of this means. If whatever the worker claims has happened is something recognized under worker's compensation, or something which a court can be convinced should be recognized under worker's compensation, then the employer can escape liability altogether.

Nothing, of course, is really ever so simple, because worker's compensation insurance premiums are often based on loss experience. An increase in claims exposure will translate into additional expense at some point down the line, but the savings are still substantial in being able to treat any particular claim as a worker's compensation claim rather than as grounds for a civil suit.

Unfortunately, there is a wide disparity among individual state systems as to the degree to which they recognize effects of on-the-job stress as compensable under worker's compensation. Under some systems, effects of stress, such as hypertension, heart problems, ulcers, nervous tension, phobias, panic disorders and all sorts of psychiatric conditions, are compensable under worker's compensation if the claimant can relate them to the stress of the job.

Other states follow the rule that occupational illnesses must be disorders which are peculiar to the employee's specific occupation and not things which are endemic in the employment relationship itself or common facts of life outside the workplace. Under this interpretation of occupational illness, the term would apply to black lung disease suffered by underground miners or nerve damage in the hands of carpenters or other workers who use hand-held power tools. It would not apply to lung disease from second-hand cigarette smoke, or back problems from sitting in an office chair, since these are not peculiar to a particular occupation or things which necessarily happen on the job as opposed to other places.

The latter interpretation of occupational illness would probably not include on-the-job stress, since stress, even if it is caused by the job, is not something peculiar to specific occupations. It is also not something which is inherent in the workplace as opposed to the ordinary affairs of life outside the parameters of the job.

It should come as no surprise that worker's compensation premiums are noticeably higher where the former rather than the latter treatment of on-the-job stress is in force. Despite the fact that certain benefits do accrue to the employer due to the immunity from negligence suits from employees, employers' organizations have always been active in legislative efforts to restrict the scope of worker's compensation benefits.

An employer in a particular jurisdiction may not have a choice whether a particular claim will be recognized as compensable under the state's worker's compensation system. Nevertheless, it is important to investigate how the system works in the particular jurisdiction where the employer is situated, as it is usually beneficial to treat stress claims as worker's compensation claims if at all possible.

The employer might prefer to have the claim treated as something not recognized under worker's compensation, because in many circumstances the employer will be able to defeat an on-the-job stress claim altogether if the matter goes to court rather than being left for determination within the worker's compensation system. In order to make a sober assessment of the employer's chance of prevailing, it is important to understand how the courts will view these claims. In many cases the employer will have a good chance of winning if the case is vigorously defended.

The law makes a very basic distinction between negligence and intentional conduct when civil courts must determine the fate of parties accused of wrongful conduct which causes injuries to others. Negligence is doing something which an ordinarily prudent person would not do, or omitting to do something an ordinarily prudent person would do under the circumstances. Intentional conduct involves the specific intention to produce harm to the victim.

Negligent Conduct

Courts in the United States widely hold to the principle that liability for negligence does not include payment for the consequences of purely emotional or psychic factors, if there has been no actual physical injury to the party bringing the suit.

All sorts of wrongs, which do not produce bodily injury, have an emotional or psychic dimension, which the law in the United States simply does not compensate. Car accidents where no one is injured are very distressing, as are breach of contract cases in business settings, disputes with landlords, consumer complaints over shoddy products and incompetent services, and on and on and on. Where no one is injured, only the "hard" costs, what the law terms special damages, can be recovered in civil court.

If the party has not suffered a direct physical injury on the job, the party cannot claim damages from the employer for what the law would term negligent infliction of emotional distress. This is simply because the law does not recognize negligent infliction of emotional distress as compensable in civil court. If the party has sustained a physical injury, however, the case is not compensable in civil court because worker's compensation comes into the picture as the sole remedy permitted by law, and the employer is immune from suit for on-the-job injuries, under basic principles of worker's compensation law.

This means that on-the-job stress cases, where the party bringing the suit alleges that the employer negligently caused psychic trauma which resulted in stress, even if the stress in turn has led to bodily manifestations, will not succeed.

The only instances where on-the-job stress claims are succeeding in civil court are the rare instances where the employee can prove successfully that intentional infliction of emotional distress has occurred. Intentional infliction of emotional distress, in legal jargon, means not only that the employer's conduct was intentional, but that the conduct was intentionally meant to cause the employee in question to suffer because of it.

Intentional Conduct

It should be pointed out that any form of illegal discrimination, on the basis of race, gender, age, national origin, marital status, pregnancy, handicap, religion, as well as sexual harassment, which violates employees' recognized civil rights, is considered intentional conduct for which consideration will be taken in awarding damages. These topics are developed more fully in other separate chapters of this book. This chapter examines cases where an employer, manager, supervisor, or coworker with tacit support from management, does something to an employee which is intended to inflict distress upon that person and which does not specifically amount to discrimination or harassment on the basis of those specific factors referred to above which are recognized under state and federal civil rights laws.

When intentional infliction of emotional distress is alleged in a civil suit, the party bringing the suit must overcome a threshold requirement before the suit can succeed. The threshold requirement will be explained to the jury in terms of what the law refers to as "outrage." The jury will be instructed that the law states that intentional infliction of emotional distress is recoverable only if the alleged wrongful conduct of the alleged party at fault fits the legal definition of outrage. In addition, no damages can be awarded unless the jury finds that the defendant's conduct is legally "outrageous," that is, so extreme in character as to fall well outside the bounds of decency and is utterly intolerable in civilized society.

When the jury is instructed that only "outrageous" conduct, in the legal sense, is compensable, it is no wonder that most verdicts in these cases exonerate the employer, or any other party, for that matter, alleged to have committed intentional infliction of emotional distress, assuming that discrimination or civil-rights-related harassment has not taken place. The law recognizes that in the give and take of everyday life people will cause a good deal of distress to their fellows, which the law will not be burdened with having to deal with except in the most extreme cases of intentional outrageous conduct.

It should further be noted that the law gives employers a qualified legal privilege where matters of discipline are concerned. It allows employers to investigate and interrogate employees about matters of legitimate employer interest, such as the physical security of the employer's premises and the loyalty and fidelity of employees who handle valuable assets belonging to the employer, despite the fact that these will almost always be very distressing situations for those involved.

The employer is free to conduct disciplinary and investigative activities as long as these activities are carried out only to further the employer's legitimate interests and are not used merely as a pretext to harass or embarrass certain individuals. The only restraints are statutes which specifically outlaw wiretapping, electronic surveillance, lie detector tests, and breaking and entering employee's personal cars and private residences. It is also illegal for parties who are not police officers to detain others by use or threat of force without evidence that a crime has just been committed or is being committed in the immediate vicinity where the person is sought to be detained.

The only emotional distress cases which do succeed are those where an employee is the victim of on-the-job harassment which serves no legitimate purpose, but is only an expression of the employer's, manager's, or supervisor's hostile or vindictive personal feelings toward the employee, or cases where there is a violation of an employee's rights by criminal conduct on the employer's or a supervisor's part. Management naturally has to be alert for potential situations of this nature, because under principles of vicarious liability the organization will most likely be liable for what the manager or supervisor has done, assuming the manager's or supervisor's conduct bears some relationship to the job.

If an employee is forced to resign due to illegal harassment on the job, the law will treat it as if the employee has been wrongfully discharged. This can open the employer up to liability for loss of income and benefits, loss of future earnings potential, damage to the employee's reputation, as well as intangible factors such as mental anguish and emotional distress. Whether or not the employee has been terminated or constructively terminated in this fashion, damages in these cases will include a large component of emotional or psychic distress, which may very well manifest itself in physical symptoms or in medically-recognized psychiatric disturbances which can have far-reaching consequences.

Any time intentional conduct comes into play, the courts in most U.S. jurisdictions will consider an award of punitive damages to punish the employer and to deter it and others from repeating the same sort of conduct. As if the purely compensatory components of the awards in these cases are not large enough, punitive damages are usually many times the compensatory component.

As a footnote, when employees complain of stress on the job and seek financial compensation, since this is rarely directly the legal responsibility of the employer, what employees are most often after is disability insurance benefits. Many disability policies recognize stress as a disabling condition, if the employee can establish his or her disability on the basis of stress with medical or psychiatric evidence. Under the particular policy in question it may not be relevant whether the stress has been caused by the job, although that will most likely be the most significant cause of stress in the lives of most disability insurance claimants.

Employers should consider carefully the cost and benefits of providing disability insurance, and, specifically, disability insurance which compensates employees who can successfully prove they are disabled due to stress. This insurance is enormously expensive, and the employer's premiums, for larger employers, may take the employer's individual loss experience into consideration. On the other hand, the availability of such insurance might take some of the heat off the employer and place the onus on the disability insurer to handle, adjust, and pay on-the-job stress claims.

Conclusion

Although on-the-job stress cases are rarely successful in producing verdicts against the employer, those which do fit the very narrow categorization which the law will permit to succeed often produce verdicts with catastrophic implications for the employer's continued operations. Thus, it is very important for business owners, executives, managers, and supervisors to become thoroughly familiar with the law in this area.

Chapter Seven

Drug and Alcohol Testing

Drug and alcohol testing and screening of employees are relatively new issues in personnel management and have come into widespread use only since the mid-1970s. When management began insisting on testing and screening, employees began filing lawsuits, and the court system was called upon to frame a coherent response which would outline the prerogatives of management and define the rights of employees in this hotly contested area. Fortunately the courts responded quickly, and there is now a more or less uniform body of case precedents available which, if interpreted properly, will give management concrete advice as to how employers may proceed where drug and alcohol testing and screening are concerned.

The issues in this area are sometimes divided between questions about drug and alcohol testing and questions concerning drug and alcohol screening. Testing occurs when the employer singles out a particular individual, usually in response to suspicion generated by the individual's conduct under specific circumstances or general overall demeanor, which suggest drug or alcohol abuse is going on. For example, an employee involved in an accident which suggests the employee was intoxicated, an employee who appears intoxicated, hung-over or impaired, or an employee observed drinking or

67

taking drugs on the job, might be given a chemical or biological assay to ascertain that substance abuse is actually taking place before disciplinary or other corrective measures are undertaken.

Screening, on the other hand, involves subjecting employees to drug and alcohol assays without any particular suspicion or specific cause to believe that substance abuse is taking place. Screening might be incorporated into the employee's pre-employment physical examination and subsequent examinations, or the employer may just decide that everyone needs to be evaluated biologically for possible substance abuse, on a one-shot or periodic basis.

Employers have a great deal of latitude under the law to subject their employees to testing or screening. Although to the lay person there might seem to be a major difference between testing and screening, there is none where the law is concerned. Therefore, the term "testing" will be used in place of both testing and screening since the law, under the most recent and most persuasive precedents, makes no distinction as far as employers' prerogatives are concerned.

When we state that the employer may "require" an employee to submit to drug or alcohol testing, it is important to note that the employer cannot actually force anyone to do anything against his or her will. This also assumes that the employer is not operating under a court order and has no special powers usually invested only in the police and special governmental investigative agencies. Any time it is indicated that the employer may require something in the area of drug and alcohol testing, it means only that the employer may demand it as an essential condition of continued employment and nothing more.

One widely held misconception is that there is a fundamental difference, legally speaking, between what employees do at work and what they do on their own time. Presumably the employee bargains away only his or her working time for the compensation agreed upon with the employer, and the employee is responsible to the employer only for his or her conduct and performance during the specific hours he or she is on the job. The other side of the coin, as the argument goes, is that when the employee is not working, the employee is free, as far as the relationship with the employer is concerned, to do whatever the employee sees fit, including drinking as much as is desired and using whatever drugs in whatever quantities the employee might choose.

The legal principles accepted by the courts in these cases make it clear that the employee's conduct both on and off the job can, at the employer's discretion, become a legitimate subject of employer concern. The employer can make off-the-job conduct an essential term of the employment relationship, just as much as conduct on the job, unless the employee has the bargaining power to force the issue the other way.

It is widely held that the impairment caused by episodic drug and alcohol use, as well as the progressive deterioration suffered when chronic drug and alcohol abuse come into the picture, do not make neat distinctions between off-the-job conduct and on-the-job performance. What employees do off the job does affect their work, as much as those caught up in the vicious cycle of substance abuse may not want to admit it.

Legally, however, this is all really quite irrelevant, because under our system employers are not required to justify their demands upon their employees on these or other grounds. The law in the United States is that an employee, in the absence of a specific employment contract or labor/management collective bargaining agreement, is an employee at will, meaning that the employee can quit, and the employer can discharge the employee at any time for any reason. Similarly, assuming there is no individual employment contract or union bargaining agreement, the terms and conditions of employment are always subject to continual redefinition and renegotiation between the employer and the employee.

Without a contract or bargaining agreement, if the employer tries to impose drug and alcohol testing, or, for that matter, any other change in the terms and conditions of employment, the employee is free to accept the change, negotiate with the employer over it, quit, or be fired for refusal to comply. The same is true for employer policies regarding use or restraint from use of drugs or alcohol, on or off the job, apart from the question of actual testing. Testing, however, would probably be a concomitant integral part of such a prohibitionary program.

The exceptions which the courts have recognized to the rule of employment at will, as expansive as they have become, have not come to include drug and alcohol use or abuse or refusal to submit to testing. Discrimination on the basis of race, religion, age, gender, national origin, pregnancy, handicap, and marital status, on the other hand, have been very strictly outlawed as permissible grounds for making employment decisions.

Discrimination based on alcohol or drug use, however, carries no adverse legal consequences. The law of wrongful discharge based on employer retaliation has not been extended to cover drug or alcohol use or abuse. Drinking and drug use are not forms of conduct which the law seeks to afford special legal protection. Discrimination and retaliatory discharge are developed in detail in other chapters of this book.

The courts have held uniformly that where a union collective bargaining agreement is in place or under negotiation, the subject of drug and alcohol testing is to be resolved under the principles of labor law. If management wants testing, the union and management must treat management's demand like others which arise in the course of negotiations, and bargain in good faith over it as required by law. Drug and alcohol testing are no different than other issues arising in contract negotiations covering wages, benefits, hours, work rules, discipline, and discharge.

Once the specific parameters of testing are incorporated into a collective bargaining agreement and properly ratified by management and the union, those parameters become part of the everyday work rules in the shop. Disputes must be ironed out in the give-and-take of grievance procedures as outlined in the agreement, under procedures provided by the National Labor Relations Act or applicable state law for state employees.

As a general proposition, under federal and state labor law, disputes over garden-variety work issues, including drug and alcohol testing, cannot be taken to court except under extreme cases. Once a collective bargaining agreement is in place there are almost always low-level grievance procedures, and then further appeals within the company and union hierarchy, with increasing levels of formality, until the controversy, whatever it happens to be, is handed over to an outside mediator or is eventually decided in binding arbitration.

If a dispute with an employee over drug and alcohol testing is taken to court, with the employee seeking damages from the employer for illegal or otherwise wrongful conduct on the employer's part, and there is a collective bargaining agreement in force which covers the issue of drug and alcohol testing, the court, if it is prepared to rule correctly, will dismiss the case and throw the employee out of court. The courts are not allowed to intervene in labor/management controversies covered by collective bargaining, whatever the merits of the case may be.

In fact, the policy of judicial nonintervention into matters covered by collective bargaining under the National Labor Relations Act is so strong that state courts are required to defer jurisdiction to federal courts, simply on the basis that a state court cannot decide matters of federal law in this arena. And the federal court, of course, is ninety-nine percent sure to refuse involvement in the case, on the basis that grievance procedures, mediation, and arbitration are the sole remedies where there is a collective bargaining agreement.

Thus, employers in union shops who are faced with suits or threats of suits over drug and alcohol testing issues, assuming the agreement with the union covers the subject, may have to go through a lengthy grievance process and accept a potentially unfavorable ruling in arbitration, but they do not have much in the way of exposure to damages suits in civil court.

Constitutional Rights of Employment Relationships

A further widely-held misconception is that drug or alcohol testing is an invasion of privacy which violates the rights we all hold under the Constitution and Bill of Rights to freedom from unwarranted searches and seizures. In order to address this issue, it is necessary to distinguish between private and public sector employments. Actually there are three categories of employment relationships where the question of constitutional rights arises, purely private employers, purely public employers, that is, government agencies, and "quasi-public" employers, technically in the private sector, which are comprehensively regulated by mandatory governmental regulations.

Purely Private Employers

Where purely private employers are concerned, constitutional rights do not come into play. The Constitution and Bill of Rights, with certain exceptions which are not relevant here, only protect persons from the actions of governmental entities and parties acting under governmental authority. Governmental authority means authority to carry out the public police power, not just authority to do what the law permits private parties to do to further their own interests. Private parties, persons, or corporations, again with certain exceptions not relevant here, cannot violate the constitutional rights of anyone.

For example, a landlord who enters and searches a tenant's apartment for a cat or dog not permitted under the lease, or a hotel keeper who enters a guest's room and seizes the guest's luggage in lieu of payment of the bill, may or may not be acting within the bounds of special authority given to them by law. If not, they may be subject to suit for illegal entry or conversion of private property or to criminal prosecution for burglary. But whether or not they have stayed strictly within the bounds of a legal privilege, they are not acting as police, and thus will never be subject to civil suit for violation of constitutional rights.

Private employers, assuming they are not forcing an employee but are merely requiring that an employee submit to testing as a condition of continued employment, are authorized to conduct drug and alcohol testing of their employees. They are likewise immune to charges of violation of constitutional rights, because, whether or not their conduct is appropriate, it is not an exercise of public police power, and thus not something to which the Constitution and Bill of Rights ever were meant to apply.

Purely Public Employers

Public employers, on the municipal, county, state, and federal levels, on the other hand, are governmental agencies, and the Constitution and Bill of Rights do apply to how they treat their employees. It may seem anomalous that public employees, who, if anything, should be more strictly accountable for their behavior than the rest

addiction and chemical dependency are disabilities for which an employee cannot be discriminated against. Intoxication and resulting impairment of performance can be a subject for discipline, but the employee with an underlying addiction or dependency, who recognizes his or her problem and wants help, may be considered a disabled person whose needs must be accommodated under state law in some jurisdictions.

Successfully rehabilitated illegal drug users are protected from discrimination under the Americans With Disabilities Act of 1990, effective July 1992, but active substance use is afforded no legal protection. The Act does not interfere in any way with employers' prerogatives where alcohol and drug testing are concerned.

To the extent drug and alcohol addiction or dependency are not treated as disabilities under local or federal law, the employer can discipline or discharge the employee consistently with the individual employment contract or collective bargaining agreement in force.

Conclusion

Employers enjoy a wide range of freedom to implement policies and procedures designed with a view toward a drug and alcohol free workplace, and even, if they want, drug and alcohol free employees on and off the job. They must be guided by concerns over employee's reputations, may not unfairly brand anyone as a drug or alcohol user or abuser, and must be careful how such information is handled. Administration of drug and alcohol tests themselves should be regulated to insure fairness and freedom from potential embarrassment or abuse.

Chapter Eight

Smoking

Smoking is an emotionally charged issue in our society. Health advocates are constantly reminding us of various rationales that exist for condemning the once widely accepted practice of smoking tobacco. These range from the sickening smell of stale smoke which lingers in cars, rooms, and other places where smokers smoke, to serious medical concerns over the almost inevitable chronic heart and respiratory illnesses smokers often must endure, and to the brutal prospect of suffering and dying from lung cancer which a substantial portion of smokers will eventually face.

Second-hand smoke is, in many ways, a more highly charged issue than smoking itself, in that it involves the rights of other persons who are subjected involuntarily to the noxious and toxic effects of smokers' smoking. Smokers presumably are at liberty in a free society to smoke if they want, but they are not at liberty to infect the rest of the people with the poisonous by-products emanating from their own cigarette smoke.

Smokers' Rights

Employers in some contexts are facing questions over banning direct cigarette consumption by their employees altogether, on and off the job, and wondering whether this comports with their employees' legal rights. In the arena of employment law, however, the smoking issue most often boils down to the conflict of "smokers' rights" versus the rights of nonsmokers to be free from exposure to the noxious effects of second-hand cigarette smoke in the workplace.

The issue of "smokers' rights" can be disposed of rather summarily. Smokers have no rights, at least as far as smoking is concerned. Smokers simply do not have the right to smoke, and employers do not have to allow them to smoke or accommodate their need or desire to smoke in the workplace.

Employers' Rights

Employers are also free to make adverse employment decisions, in hiring, firing, transfers, promotions or whatever else, based on whether or not a particular employee smokes, on or off the job. Vocal proponents of "smokers' rights" may complain that employment discrimination arises from differential treatment of smokers, but as will become clear in the other chapters of this book dealing with issues in employment discrimination law, discrimination is only illegal when it is based on certain well-defined classifications such as race, gender, age, pregnancy, and marital status. The rule of employment at will is in full force and effect in most other contexts.

In fact, smoking is rapidly coming to be seen as a manifestation of deviance associated with persons with low levels of educational and vocational attainment. Among persons who should know better than to smoke, smoking is coming to be seen as a form of substance abuse behavior for which intervention, counselling, and treatment are regarded as appropriate strategies to bring about cessation of this habit. Just as with more obvious forms of substance abuse such as excessive drinking and illegal use of drugs, employee behavior on and off the job are legitimate areas of employer concern. Employers for one reason or another may wish to refuse to hire smokers, require them to quit smoking to keep their jobs, and do so without regard to whether smoking occurs at work, at home or elsewhere.

Employees who smoke, wherever they smoke, are widely thought to suffer more medical problems than nonsmokers. In addition to the catastrophic consequences of contracting emphysema, heart disease, or lung cancer, smokers are believed to have a greater incidence of common illnesses like colds and flu. This all directly translates into absenteeism and lost productivity, whether or not smokers are also wasting time lighting up on the job, going outside to smoke, or sneaking off to the bathroom. Group insurance rates are lower for nonsmoking groups, or at least for groups comprised only of nonsmokers and former smokers who have successfully quit.

However, as compelling as the reasons an employer may have for restricting or banning employee smoking altogether, evaluation of the adequacy of the employer's reasons for conducting an anti-smoking campaign or for banning smoking on or off the job is legally irrelevant. This was explained in the discussion of employee alcohol and drug use both in the workplace and on the employee's own time. Under the rule of employment at will, where no employment contract is in force, and as long as the employer does not make decisions about employees or prospective employees based on impermissible categorizations related to race, gender, age, nationality, marital status, pregnancy, and other factors recognized under antidiscrimination law, or make decisions with a retaliatory motivation as delineated in the material on retaliatory discharge, the employer is free to hire, fire, discipline, and promote or refuse to promote based on whatever factors the employer deems relevant. And similarly, of course, the employee is free at any time, in the absence of an employment contract stipulating otherwise, to quit for any reason, including the employee's dissatisfaction over the employer's policies relating to smoking.

Protecting the Rights of Nonsmokers

Actually the law has gone beyond this to a certain degree in protecting the rights of nonsmokers. There is such a thing emerging as "nonsmokers' rights." The most salient developments in the protection of nonsmokers from second-hand smoke have come not in the arena of litigation but in the legislative and administrative context.

In some jurisdictions there now are relatively new statutes and regulations which forbid smoking outright in the workplace or which severely restrict it to outdoor areas or indoor areas physically separated from the general nonsmoking environment. Smokers in other jurisdictions still have one right left, and that is the right of every citizen to influence the actions of their elected representatives when it comes to voting down restrictions on smoking in the workplace. In many areas attempts at banning or restricting smoking in the workplace have been unsuccessful, in part because of misdirected respect for "smokers' rights," but more likely because smokers are simply able to muster enough votes to keep such legislation from gaining a foothold in the communities where they live and work.

Much of the antismoking legislation now in effect is a matter of local municipal action, in specific geographical locales, often urban areas or places with more liberal or progressive political traditions than the rest of the country. Most places, and the majority of states at the state level, have not picked up on the fashionable contemporary trend toward smoking as deviant rather than mainstream behavior, and still allow it as a matter of individual choice.

Employers should be alert for local laws which may restrict smoking on the job, because if such laws are in effect where they happen to do business and they do not adhere to both the spirit and the letter of the law, they can expect an immediate, vocal and likely highly litigious response from antismoking forces.

Smoking has also been attacked in court in individual cases brought by disaffected nonsmokers against employers who have not restricted on-the-job smoking by coworkers, thus subjecting these disaffected individuals to the noxious effects of second-hand smoke and leading them to sue for damages. Until recently, these cases have been largely unsuccessful primarily in jurisdictions which do not have specific legislative or administrative enactments which directly outlaw smoking in the workplace.

Cases Dealing with Smoking

Employers who wish to permit smoking or who do not wish to deal with the potential problems associated with banning it are entitled to be aware of the manner in which the courts have ruled in unsuccessful attempts by disaffected nonsmokers. These forces have tried to use the civil courts to obtain compensation, to strike back at employers who have not been willing to restrict coworkers from smoking and to obtain precedential rulings as a vehicle to enforce nonsmoking policies prospectively in the workplace.

One rationale nonsmoking employees have sought to use in litigation is the argument that their employers have, in individual cases, agreed contractually to provide, at least to them if not to everyone, a smoke-free workplace. In general terms, an employment contract need not be set down specifically in writing to be enforceable, but it can arise from oral assurances or even a certain course of conduct between the parties. Although this rationale has not been used successfully by a disaffected employee under the facts of any reported case decision of which this author is aware, it would seem that this rationale could very likely be used successfully in any situation where an employee is promised or led to believe he or she was coming into a smoke-free workplace, and then left to suffer from exposure to second-hand smoke.

Although there is no known case precedent which actually says this, if an employer, as many employers now are doing, sets up a policy that the workplace will be smoke-free, the employer should be bound to see that that policy is maintained and enforced, or face the prospect of breach-of-contract litigation from employees who felt they had bargained for a smoke-free working environment as part of their agreed-upon compensation package. Again, since there is no known actual case precedent presently on the books, it is difficult to anticipate how the court would assess damages against the employer for such breach of contract if breach of contract is established in this type of case. Nevertheless, the possibilities which this scenario presents should bear some consideration by thoughtful business owners, executives, managers, and personnel specialists.

Another rationale advanced only unsuccessfully by antismoking forces is that there is a common-law duty owed by employers to provide a smoke-free workplace for their employees. In the absence of an actual statute or administrative regulation, the courts which have considered this issue explicitly have not yet found employers to have such a common-law duty. Presumably where there is an actual statute or regulation specifically circumscribing employer practices regarding smoking, the courts will not have to discuss whether or not a common-law duty exists, given that there would be a clearly articulated legislative policy to guide the courts in making such a decision without resort to common-law principles.

Perhaps one of the most interesting cases for lawyers and foreboding cases for employers who do not wish to confront the smoking issue in the workplace has been a case recently handed down by the Supreme Court of the State of Washington. It involved an office worker who sued her employer for respiratory problems allegedly caused by exposure to second-hand smoke on the job. The case is interesting to lawyers because it involves a novel application of rather complex technical legal rules to a common factual situation. Until the case was actually decided, it was one which lawyers might dismiss as a case where the disaffected party simply had no legal remedy. This should alert those not trained in legal analysis that the discussion immediately following, although it deals with a very simple factual scenario, may be somewhat difficult to follow from a legal standpoint.

The decisive question legally was whether or not exposure to second-hand smoke was an occupational illness compensable under worker's compensation or industrial insurance. Worker's compensation and industrial insurance are two widely used terms for the same thing, a system in effect in one form or another in all U.S. jurisdictions in which the effects of on-the-job injuries and occupational illnesses, (that is, medical expenses, time loss, rehabilitation and some compensation for permanent partial and permanent total disability) are paid on a no-fault basis by the employer, the employer's insurer, or the state depending on the local system in force.

The general trade-offs given to employers by society requiring them to submit to the worker's compensation or industrial insur-

Chapter Nine

An Introduction to Antidiscrimination Law

Topics which fall under the ambit of antidiscrimination law are affected by a combination of state and federal laws. Acts of employment discrimination on the basis of race, gender, national origin, and religion are outlawed by the Civil Rights Act of 1964, the basic federal legislation on the subject of discrimination which covers not only employment but many other facets of our national life. Age discrimination is covered by the 1978 Age Discrimination in Employment Act. Until passage of the Americans With Disabilities Act of 1990, effective July 1992, disability discrimination was not covered by a comprehensive federal statute or regulatory scheme, but was nevertheless outlawed under state law in many U.S. jurisdictions.

Regulations and court precedents against sexual harassment, marital status discrimination, and pregnancy discrimination grew out of the gender-based antidiscrimination provisions of Title VII of the 1964 Civil Rights Act. These are now considered by some to be separate subjects apart from gender-based discrimination and are treated in their own separate chapters of this book. The law in these areas began with the 1964 Civil Rights Act, but state laws in many states also took up the cause and are now an important practical factor in how any particular controversy in these areas is likely to be resolved.

State and Federal Law

Not every state even has a law on the books covering each potential area of discrimination, although most states do outlaw discrimination based on race, gender, religion, age, and national origin. Some have laws, especially in the area of racial discrimination, which predate the 1964 Civil Rights Act by many years.

On the other hand, some states and localities outlaw forms of discrimination which are not recognized on the federal level, such as discrimination based on political and sexual preferences, HIV infection and AIDS, and treat these and the more conventional forms of discrimination such as race, age, sex, religion, and national origin much more severely than they are treated by the federal government under federal law.

To understand the complex interplay of state and federal forces at work in antidiscrimination law, it is necessary to briefly review the basics of how our federal system is made up. It should go without saying that federal law is paramount under our constitutional system, and that federal law is the same, more or less, throughout the country. State law, on the other hand, is generally considered subordinate to federal law, and is different in each state.

Under our federal system the states are the basic unit of government since the thirteen original colonies existed and operated independently before the federal government was formed. Under the constitution, however, certain spheres of authority have been irrevocably given to the federal government by the states. One of the best example is the power of the federal government to regulate interstate commerce.

Federal antidiscrimination laws are an exercise of the power of the federal government to regulate interstate commerce. The Thirteenth and Fourteenth Amendments to the Constitution also give the federal government enforcement powers in the area of racial discrimination, but the basic wellspring of federal authority against employment discrimination is still the Interstate Commerce Clause of the U.S. Constitution.

The regulation of interstate commerce is an area of supreme federal authority under the Constitution. In some contexts, for example licensing and taxation of vehicles used in interstate trade, the states can pass their own laws as long as they do not interfere with what was set down by the federal authorities. However, in other contexts, like flight operations at airports, states are not allowed to get involved at all, whether or not state law would be compatible with laws and regulations enacted on the federal level. The situation where the federal government takes over and entirely dominates the field is referred to as federal pre-emption.

In the area of antidiscrimination law, the intent of Congress has been that there be no federal pre-emption of the field. This enables states to enact their own laws and set up their own procedures to cover the subject of discrimination in employment, as long as the states are not more lenient with the subject of discrimination than the federal government has chosen to be. The states are not dependent upon the federal government for their authority. States can enact any antidiscrimination laws they want, as long as their laws are as stringent as federal law, and the laws do not attempt to relax the provisions of comparable federal laws, and do not somehow infringe on individual liberties guaranteed by the Bill of Rights.

It is important to recognize that although state laws vary, federal law will always apply to the employer's conduct, assuming the employer has enough employees to be covered. This generally means having more than 15 employees. And federal law is basically the same throughout the country, although local federal agencies may vary in a number of areas. These areas might include the degree of activism staff members share and their willingness to work informally with employers, rather than trying to make public examples of untoward employer practices.

In the past there have been differences in how the antidiscrimination laws were interpreted by the local federal courts in different parts of the country. A federal district court must follow the precedents of the federal circuit court of appeals which governs the particular part of the country where the district court is located. Federal circuit courts, however, do not have to follow precedents from other federal circuit courts. They are only responsible to the U.S. Supreme Court for the correctness of their rulings. There have been at times major differences in how the same federal laws have been applied in different federal judicial circuits around the country. This continued until the Supreme Court had a case appropriate for it to use to set down a uniform national precedent on the issue in question. As disconcerting as this may appear, it is not presently a problem in the area of federal antidiscrimination law.

As a practical matter, every state is a little bit different in what its laws provide and in how they operate. Recognizing and understanding that there are common patterns in interpretation between the federal and state levels and among different states' laws will be very helpful to the practical-minded business owner, manager, or executive who may be feeling a little bit overwhelmed at this point.

It should be obvious that business owners, executives, managers, and personnel professionals have to consult with knowledgeable local legal counsel for answers to specific questions in the area of state antidiscrimination law. This chapter can only discuss general principles of how the laws operate. It can alert the reader to issues which are likely to be important in handling discrimination claims on a day-to-day basis in the workplace.

The differences between federal and state laws are in many respects based on procedure rather than substantive law. This means that in addition to the difference between the content or substance of the laws, there are procedural differences in how the law is enforced. This includes whether enforcement is brought about by governmental agencies or by private parties who feel they have been victims of discriminatory employment practices and policies.

On the federal level, enforcement is carried out by the Equal Employment Opportunity Commission (EEOC). The EEOC hears and determines the validity of discrimination charges brought against employers, as well as serves as an advocate in federal court for parties which it determines to have been victimized by employers' discriminatory conduct. If the EEOC is unable to obtain compliance with a determination it makes that discrimination has taken place and that certain remedial action is warranted, the EEOC is authorized to sue in federal court to bring about the desired result if the employer is not able or willing to accede to the EEOC's position voluntarily.

Private parties are able to file charges of employer discrimination for hearing before the EEOC. If the EEOC does not reach a favorable determination and either brings about employer compliance or sues in federal court on the party's behalf within a relatively short period of time, the party is able to sue the employer in his or her own right in federal court.

The remedies for parties proceeding under federal law include remedial orders. Orders may come from the EEOC, which has no enforcement power of its own except the authority to sue in federal court, or from the federal courts, which conceivably have all of the power of the federal government behind them. Orders typically call for employers to alter their discriminatory practices relative to future conduct and to place victims of past discrimination in the same place they would now be in if discrimination had not taken place. This includes making sure job advancement, back pay, salary increases and back benefits are compensated. The party or parties going before the EEOC or directly into federal court seeking to rectify employer discriminatory practices may be individuals, small groups of employees, or even a large class of individuals (such as all past and present female employees of a particular employer who have suffered from differential hiring and promotional practices).

Administrative Agencies

Administrative remedies, under the EEOC or state equal employment opportunity commissions or comparable agencies, are used when the employee or group of employees want to alter the existing relationship with the employer, which has been tainted with discrimination, and go on living with the arrangement after it has been purged of the effects of past discrimination and rectified by judicial assurances that discrimination will not take place in the future. Or a disaffected job seeker or group of job seekers may simply want to be hired or at least considered on a non-discriminatory basis.

The reason administrative agencies have been set up in this context is that they are considered the governmental format best suited to resolving complex situations and applying technically detailed statutes and regulations to what can become enormously complicated factual patterns. Administrative agencies combine the functions of the legislature, executive, and judiciary branches. They promulgate their own rules and regulations which define the actual substance of the law. They then bring about enforcement of the law and their own regulations, first by adjudicating how controversies are to be resolved and then by bringing suit in court to enforce or to defend the agency's position.

Administrative agencies are upheld in court most of the time. The policy of the law is to promote administrative resolutions of controversies entrusted to the special competence of administrative agencies operating within their particular provinces. When appearing before an administrative agency or working with it to resolve a particular controversy in the area of employment discrimination, no one should be misled by the informality of the agency's processes or by the lack of the usual trappings of judicial authority.

As a practical matter the resolution which an administrative agency comes up with will be the final resolution of the questions before it. Although civil courts have the power to enforce agencies' determinations, modify agencies' findings, or even completely block them from functioning, the courts will always defer to agencies' administrative judgments unless it can be clearly shown that an agency has operated arbitrarily, is biased toward a particular party, or has ignored clearly established legal authority contrary to its position.

Under state law, there are state administrative agencies which operate much like the EEOC does on the federal level. What is probably most interesting and ominous about state law, however, is that many states allow parties to treat discrimination much the same as other common civil wrongs, like personal injuries or breach of contract. Parties can sue directly in state civil court before a jury which will assess damages against the employer.

Damages can include not only income and benefits lost due to discrimination, whether the party has not been hired, been fired, or held back from advancement, but also intangible factors. Some of these may include loss of earning capacity, mental anguish and emotional distress, psychological and psychiatric problems from the trauma of enduring discrimination, and anything else the disaffected party's lawyers can think of and get past the judge for the jury's consideration.

Punitive damages are often assessed in privately filed discrimination suits. One ostensible purpose is to deter the employer from similar conduct in the future and to serve as an example to other employers who might be engaging or considering similar acts of discrimination. Punitive damages are usually awarded, in general terms, only where there is some public interest in deterring the defendant's conduct. Civil-rights enforcement is considered to be just such an area where the public interest comes into play.

Punitive damages, unlike criminal fines, are paid directly to the prevailing party in a discrimination case. They provide additional incentive, as a pragmatic matter, to the attorney who might have taken the case on a contingent-fee basis. Punitive damages generally make it much more expensive to engage in discrimination than what is generally required to compensate the party who actually has the fortitude to file a lawsuit and carry it through to a successful conclusion.

Attorney fees are also commonly assessed against the employer in successful antidiscrimination court actions, while attorney fees are almost never assessed against an individual who brings an unsuccessful case which the jury determines to be unfounded.

Again, the prospect of an award of attorney fees, on top of compensatory and punitive damages, makes it more costly to engage in or even think about engaging in discriminatory practices. It assists the party who brings a successful case by ensuring that the party's compensation is not used up in compensating his or her legal counsel, whether or not counsel is working on an hourly or contingent-fee basis.

Awarding attorney fees in these cases is also supposed to compensate public-interest legal agencies and pro-bono attorneys. It enables them to take cases on behalf of parties who are unable to pay, or in which taking the party's award away for payment of attorney fees would defeat all but the symbolic effect of a hard-won victory.

Statutes of limitations are very short for filing under federal law, usually on the order of six months to file with the EEOC, and another six months to a year after the EEOC gets the case, depending on the complexities of just what the EEOC does or does not do with the case after that. State administrative agencies also require cases to be filed promptly after discriminatory conduct has occurred, because like the EEOC they are primarily concerned with intervening into and remedying an ongoing situation, rather than merely assessing financial compensation after the fact. Under state civil law, the statute of limitations is usually the same as for other civil wrongs, such as personal injuries, and it will range from one to three years.

Knowing that the statute of limitations for filing with the EEOC is six months, and that six months have passed and the disaffected employee has not filed legal action, may give management unwarranted cause to breathe a sigh of relief. It may only be that the employee, former employee, or dissatisfied job seeker has elected to pursue a civil suit before a jury under state law, which can often be more financially rewarding than going through the bureaucratic processes outlined under EEOC and state equal employment opportunity commission regulations.

Employers and their counsel must realize that there are many ways for employees to proceed, depending on the nature of their objectives, and that their objectives can change as the legal controversy goes on. The prospect of taking administrative action on the federal level may seem so overly complicated that the employee might not be expected to follow through with it. This may not operate to the employer's advantage, however, since there may be a much simpler administrative or judicial remedy available under state or even local law which will prove more advantageous to the employee.

An employee may have certain advantages in proceeding as an individual, or a group of employees may find it advantageous to proceed as a group. As a general observation, the larger the group of affected individuals, the more likely they will go the administrative route. Although federal and state courts have outlined in their rules procedures for class action suits, these suits are no longer widely used except where the legal position of each member of the class is virtually identical. This is almost never the case with discrimination cases where everyone is just a little bit different.

Strategies to Protect Management from Discrimination Charges

One preventative measure for employers to take is to institute personnel procedures to combat discrimination. It should be obvious that this means any decisions affecting any of the terms and conditions of employment cannot be made on discriminatory grounds. Employers should take the time and make the effort to educate all supervisory and managerial employees to just what discrimination is, how it manifests itself, and how and why it is to be eliminated.

Employers must always be in the process of preparing to defend discrimination charges and suits by making the personnel evaluation process as objective as possible all of the time. The reason for this lies in understanding how courts and administrative agencies on the federal and state levels approach the task of evaluating charges of discrimination.

First, the affected person must show that he or she has been treated differently than other individuals with respect to hiring or other terms or conditions of employment. He or she must also show that it is plausible that the employment-related decision in question was a result of discrimination on the basis of race, gender, age, religion, national origin, marital status, pregnancy, or some other classification which the local jurisdiction recognizes as impermissible grounds for employment decisions.

In evaluating charges of discrimination, the next step is for the employer to offer a legitimate basis for the personnel decision in question. For example, the employer should prove that the individual was not qualified for a particular position or for advancement, or the employee deserved the particular disciplinary action he or she received based on objective qualifications and job-performance criteria which were in existence before the adverse treatment of the individual in question actually took place. If the employer is able to show that there was an ostensibly legitimate, objective reason for the treatment the individual received, the employer will be exonerated of discrimination charges, unless the individual can demonstrate that the objective criteria upon which the employer has relied is a mere pretext to allow discrimination to have taken place.

Any time a person of one race, religion, or nationality is treated differently than a person of another, or anytime a man is treated differently than a woman, charges of discrimination are a potential consequence. If, however, the employer is able to demonstrate objective criteria for the differential treatment, the employer stands a good chance of being cleared of charges of employment discrimination. This assumes that the disaffected person is not able to carry out the difficult task of demonstrating that the employer's objective criteria are not a mere pretext for discrimination.

Certain "objective" criteria have been struck down as inherently discriminatory. Examples include nearly all age-related barriers, and physical strength, height and weight requirements which bear no relation to the job but are only designed to keep women from qualifying. These are discussed in more detail in the individual chapters dealing with separate forms of employment discrimination.

The most important strategy in protecting management from discrimination charges is to make the processes of hiring, job performance evaluations, raises, and promotions as free from subjective considerations as possible by setting down specific objective criteria and using these criteria as the basis of personnel decisions.

The process must not only be objective but must also appear objective. There have to be clear, objective criteria for hiring and promotions. Criteria should be formulated and conveyed to the employee or prospective employee before a decision is rendered and before the employee is even considered for what he or she wants. Everyone has to be treated the same with respect to the established criteria.

Subjective evaluations reflect more the attitude of the evaluator toward the person than an assessment of the employee's job performance. Subjective decisions might appear to be the employer's prerogative under the employment-at-will system, and they are, but they will prove very difficult to justify and thus stand to become very costly once a subjectively evaluated employee elects to file charges of discrimination.

Certain employees will always be the "jail house lawyers" who attempt to insulate themselves from adverse personnel decisions by complaining about real or imagined acts of job discrimination and turning personnel decision making into a kangaroo court. Unfortunately, it is as much an act of discrimination to discriminate against those who complain of discrimination as it is to discriminate in the first place, whether or not the complaints are valid. These people have to be treated with the utmost respect, and as fairly and objectively as possible, no matter how much this strains the patience of management from the lowest to the highest levels. A pragmatic approach to the problem of discrimination in the workplace will admit no other alternatives.

Chapter Ten

Age Discrimination

The law of age discrimination is often misconstrued by business and personnel managers. Keeping on the right side of laws which outlaw age discrimination is a relatively easy task, however, if employers are able to understand the law and apply it by discontinuing once widespread age discrimination practices which are now recognized as inappropriate in the contemporary workplace.

Federal and state laws both have a bearing on the subject of age discrimination. Fortunately, however, there is a good deal of uniformity between federal and state laws, at least with respect to how these laws define age-related discrimination and delineate forbidden employer practices.

Enforcement procedures differ among the states and between the state and federal level. Enforcement procedures are discussed in more detail in Chapter 9.

Federal and State Law

The basic federal law on age discrimination is the Age Discrimination in Employment Act, Title 29 United States Code, Sections 621-634, which has been amended several times since its original passage in 1967. Under the act there are detailed Equal Employment Opportunity Commission and Department of Labor regulations found in Sections 1625–1627.

The majority of states have their own laws against age discrimination in employment. They can be found by researching the law under the subject of employment discrimination or the more general heading of civil rights.

The most important point to understand is that workers aged 40 to 70 are the only persons protected by law against age discrimination in the workplace. Neither federal law nor state law is designed or intended to prevent workers younger or older than the 40- to 70-year age group from being victimized by age discrimination in employment.

The policy behind the laws against age discrimination in employment is set out explicitly in the federal statute. Congress found that older workers were becoming disadvantaged in their efforts to retain employment and were especially disadvantaged in their efforts to regain employment when displaced from their jobs. The incidence of long-term unemployment was considered a grave problem among older workers. The resultant deterioration of skills, morale, and employer acceptability presented a particular problem of unemployed older workers compared to their younger counterparts.

Arbitrary age limits without regard to job performance and employment potential had become a common practice, which obviously worked to the disadvantage of older workers. Arbitrary discrimination because of age was declared to be a burden upon interstate commerce, thus invoking the authority of Congress to pass legislation designed to prohibit arbitrary age discrimination in employment and to promote the employment of persons based on their ability rather than age.

Thus, it is only older workers, and not everyone in the workforce, who are meant to benefit from age-discrimination legislation, both on the federal and on the state levels. As odd as it may seem in relation to other facets of antidiscrimination law, age discrimination against workers younger than 40 and older than 70 is completely legal, even though many might feel that it represents an inappropriate personnel practice. It is perfectly legal to hire or promote a 20-year-old or a 45-year-old in place of a 30-year-old, on the basis of age alone, because the 30-year-old simply is not protected by the laws against age discrimination.

But it is illegal to discriminate in favor of a worker in the 40- to 70-year age bracket, when discrimination in favor of one such older worker would work against another individual in the same protected age bracket. For example, everyone would now recognize that it is illegal, assuming the decision is based on age alone, to hire or promote a 30-year-old instead of a 45-year-old, or a 30-year-old or a 45-year-old instead of a 55-year-old. But it is also illegal to hire or promote a 55-year-old instead of a 45-year-old, if the decision is based on age.

As long as the discrimination victim is in the protected 40- to 70-year age bracket, and the discrimination is based on age, the person is considered the victim of illegal discriminatory conduct on the employer's part. This is regardless of whether the discrimination actually helps another individual in the same category of older workers whom the Age Discrimination in Employment Act was meant to benefit.

The prohibition against discrimination applies not only to hiring, promotions, and wages, but also to benefits. It requires group health coverage to be available to older workers and spouses on the same basis that it is available to younger persons.

Not all employers are subject to the Federal Age Discrimination in Employment Act. Only those with twenty or more employees for each working day in each of twenty or more calendar weeks in the current or preceding calendar year are subject to the act. Note that the act makes no distinction for whether the twenty employees are part-time or full-time workers.

Employers who are subject to the federal act should be aware that in addition to observing the substance of the law against age discrimination, they are required to maintain fairly detailed records of job applications, hiring, firing, promotions, compensation paid, and the ages of the individuals involved, for a period going back three years. These data can be used by the EEOC and Department of Labor inspectors to determine whether discriminatory practices are taking place. Employers must also post notices in the workplace to inform workers of their rights against age discrimination. Local

EEOC and labor department field offices can be contacted for details.

State laws vary from state to state, but as a general rule the states do not distinguish between businesses on the basis of size or number of employees for purposes of applying their employment discrimination or civil rights laws. Thus, even if an employer is too small to be covered by the Federal Age Discrimination in Employment Act, the employer is still prevented by state law from engaging in acts of employment discrimination because of age. Business owners, executives, managers, and personnel professionals are urged to become familiar with state law on this subject.

The federal statute on age discrimination applies not only to employers but to labor organizations and employment agencies as well. Employers must be cognizant whether a union or agency from which employee referrals are obtained is engaged in discriminatory conduct aimed at older individuals. And, of course, anyone in an executive or policy-making position in a labor union or employment agency must see that the law is applied by the organization.

The EEOC has issued regulations which set out a number of specific employer practices it considers discriminatory against older workers. This is not to say that other practices are not discriminatory; only that these specific practices will likely run afoul of the law if challenged. The employer who engages in any of these specific practices will have a very difficult time justifying them on nondiscriminatory grounds.

These regulations are not binding on employers who are not covered by the Federal Age Discrimination in Employment Act. Although it is possible that a state equal employment opportunity, fair employment practices, or human rights commission could choose to apply these regulations as a matter of independent state jurisdiction over an employer not subject to the federal age discrimination legislation, by finding the regulations persuasive in denominating specific practices which any contemporary employer should consider age discriminatory.

One practice which the EEOC has declared discriminatory is the use of help wanted notices or advertisements which set forth age-related parameters for hiring. Stating that the employer is looking for someone aged 25 to 30 is obviously discriminatory, just as it is discriminatory to advertise for an individual aged 40 to 50, which is within the protected age bracket, because it would at the same time discriminate against other individuals who are protected from age discrimination.

Employers are cautioned that stating they are looking for a "young person," "recent college graduate," "boy," or "girl" is discriminatory. Less obvious, but illegal is advertising for a person "over 65" or a "retired person," since this would discriminate against many individuals in the 40- to 70-year age group who are also protected against age discrimination.

It is also recommended that help wanted advertisements not ask individuals who apply to state their ages when applying. Although there may be a legitimate reason why the employer needs to know the applicant's age during the application process or once the applicant is hired, such an advertisement will probably deter older individuals from applying and may thus prove to be discriminatory in actual practice.

Similarly, the EEOC has not ruled it automatically discriminatory to ask an individual's age in a job application, since there are legitimate reasons why the employer will need to know the employee's age and date of birth once the person has been hired, or perhaps to distinguish the applicant from others with the same name when running a background check. This practice is also frowned upon because it tends to deter older individuals from applying or following up on their applications. It could also prove to be discriminatory if someone is actually kept from applying on that basis. The EEOC has suggested that where date of birth or age are requested on an employment application, the employer include a disclaimer that the employer is prohibited by law from engaging in discriminatory employment practices relative to persons 40 to 70 years of age.

Much of the litigation surrounding age discrimination has centered on two specific issues, mandatory retirement policies, and whether arbitrary age limitations can be justified as bona fide occupational qualifications for specific jobs. Although both of these were hotly contested topics in a raft of litigated cases not very long ago, most of the litigation here can now be described in the past tense.

Mandatory Retirement

Mandatory retirement of individuals within the protected 40- to 70-year age bracket is illegal and has been illegal since the 1978 amendment to the Age Discrimination in Employment Act, except for one very limited exception. The limited exception deals with employees in executive or high policy-making positions, age 65 or older, who have held an executive or high policy-making position for at least two years before mandatory retirement is to be imposed. Individuals who fall within this limited exception can be retired involuntarily, provided they are afforded immediate annual retirement benefits of at least $44,000.00.

Bona Fide Occupational Requirements

Bona fide occupational requirements refer to the practice of setting age barriers for entry into or continued employment within particular jobs. "Bona fide" is simply Latin for "good faith." Age barriers will be sustained under the law only where the employer is able to prove that they are bona fide or good faith occupational requirements, requirements which have been set up in good faith based on objective data which demonstrate that workers older than a certain defined age are categorically unable to fulfill the legitimate requirements of the job.

This practice of setting an arbitrary age barrier for getting or keeping a certain job was once widespread, but is now likely to be found illegal on grounds of age discrimination in almost every context. The reason for this is that in most jobs in the modern workplace, human performance factors which deteriorate with age are not realistic indicators of job ability. Few jobs depend on the worker having more than a nominal degree of strength or agility, keen vision or hearing, quick reflexes, or protracted physical endurance. Many tasks in fact can be done better by older workers who bring a greater quantum of experience and judgment to the job than their younger counterparts. The courts and administrative agencies have taken notice of this fact and will look at most arbitrary age-related employment barriers as nothing more than an expression of age-related prejudice.

Most of the litigation in which specific age barriers have been allowed to stand as bona fide occupational qualifications has involved police and fire personnel and aircraft pilots. In some of these cases, the employers have been able to show the courts objective data that employees over a certain age, as a categorical matter, do not have the strength, reflexes, stamina, and endurance necessary to meet the reasonable performance expectations of the job in question.

The physical and mental demands of police patrol work, firefighting, and flying airplanes are unusually rigorous in relation to what most modern workers do to earn a living. Another important factor, however, in the police, firefighter, and pilot cases is the public importance that individuals in these jobs be in top physical and mental shape and be able to perform well under conditions of extreme stress. Because of the importance of these factors to the public, the courts, the EEOC, and state fair employment agencies will often tolerate certain older individuals losing their jobs on arbitrary age criteria who happen to be in good enough shape to keep their jobs in law enforcement, emergency response work, and in aircraft piloting. In the rest of the economy, however, employers should not expect to be able to sustain any sort of arbitrary age-related barriers as being good faith expressions of legitimate employer prerogatives rather than mere prejudice against older people.

The simplest approach to the issue of bona fide occupational qualifications for the average employer in most industries which employ office and factory assembly personnel, vehicle drivers, cooks, janitors, even construction and maintenance workers, is to assume that any arbitrary age barrier to job entry or job retention is illegal. To sustain such barriers as legally permissible requires scientific data prepared by human factors professionals able to set down objective reasons why a worker over a certain age cannot do the job under consideration. This is very difficult, in fact almost impossible in most situations and should not be attempted unless the employer is very sure of what is being done.

Now that age discrimination has been defined and specific prohibited practices have been delineated, it is important to examine what is *not* age-related discrimination. It is true that most jobs in the modern workplace are relatively easy compared to what our primitive forbears did for a living or compared to what was expected of industrial and agricultural laborers earlier this century. But there are still realistic and legitimate demands of the job which people are less able to fulfill as their age advances.

It is not illegal for the employer to maintain job performance expectations which exclude some older workers, as long as workers and potential workers of all ages are evaluated on the basis of their abilities to do the job and not on their ages alone. Any time a job performance factor has a tendency to exclude older workers, however, the employer must be able to justify the use of the performance factor on the grounds of business necessity. But it is possible to have realistic performance factors, other than outright age barriers, which will exclude some older individuals.

It requires a good deal of soul searching to determine whether prejudice or actual business necessity is the reason for such a practice. The employer must assume that any employment-related criterion which displaces or excludes older individuals will appear discriminatory and must be proven to be nondiscriminatory on the grounds that they are a business necessity, as stated in the EEOC guidelines, and not business preference or business prerogative.

Conclusion

Perhaps the employer will have to draw upon the expertise of professionals outside the law to determine whether attitudes exist within the organization which have led or will lead to prejudices against older workers. Prejudice can translate into discriminatory practices which will lead to public embarrassment and unwanted legal liability when the employer is drawn into administrative proceedings or court over age discrimination.

Chapter Eleven

Disability Discrimination

Although every state now outlaws disability discrimination in employment, enactment of the Americans With Disabilities Act of 1990 was the first comprehensive treatment of this subject on the federal level. Besides employment, the act also deals with discrimination against disabled individuals in public transportation, public accommodations and telephone service. It also requires closed-captioning of televised public-service broadcasts. Only the portions of this new legislation dealing with employment discrimination against the disabled will be discussed here.

Prior to the effective date of the Americans With Disabilities Act of 1990 in July 1992, no federal law has outlawed disability discrimination across the board in the private sector. Nevertheless, since the Rehabilitation Act of 1973, all federal government contractors have been covered by elaborate regulations which forbid discrimination by employers working on federal contracts and require affirmative action from these employers to bring disabled workers into the workplace and to train, advance, and compensate them according to their actual performance abilities. In fact, every private and public sector program or agency which receives federal funding must adhere to antidiscrimination and affirmative action guidelines mandated under the Rehabilitation Act of 1973.

Companies and agencies subject to the Rehabilitation Act are required, as a condition of obtaining federal contract assignments and funding grants, to demonstrate their familiarity with and intention and ability to comply with the nondiscrimination and affirmative action guidelines of the particular subunits of the federal government with which they happen to be dealing.

Discussing these regulations in detail for the benefit of prospective federal contractors and for programs seeking federal funding is beyond the scope of this book. Agencies as diverse as the Postal Service, Department of Transportation, Small Business Administration, Department of Health and Human Services, National Foundation on the Arts and Humanities and many, many others each have their own individual regulations covering disability discrimination and affirmative action by contractors and grant recipients. These were put into effect to comply with the Rehabilitation Act of 1973.

The Americans with Disabilities Act

The Americans with Disabilities Act of 1990, on the other hand, applies to all employers in the United States in industries affecting commerce, with fifteen or more employees for each working day in each of twenty or more calendar weeks in the current or preceding calendar year. With the exception of smaller employers who are not covered, the act is meant to outlaw disability discrimination across the board in the private sector of the U.S. economy. The phrase "industries affecting commerce" is only a technicality which serves to invoke the jurisdiction of the U.S. Government under the Interstate Commerce Clause of the U.S. Constitution, and does not, for practical purposes, exclude any employer from the reach of the act's provisions.

The Americans With Disabilities Act of 1990 is premised on certain Congressional findings. A review of the legislative findings of Congress will help employers to understand the purpose of the act and of state legislation designed to benefit disabled workers and to anticipate the thrust enforcement action is likely to take in the courts and on the administrative level. In understanding any law, the place to start is to review the stated motivation of the legislature in enacting it.

Historically, it has been found that society has tended to isolate and segregate individuals with disabilities. Despite some improvements, disability discrimination remains a pervasive social problem which has lagged behind other forms of discrimination in the availability of effective legal recourse for affected individuals. Persons with disabilities are a discreet and insular minority who have been faced with restrictions and limitations. They have been subjected to a history of unequal treatment and relegated to a position of inferiority, based on characteristics beyond their control and stereotyped assumptions not truly indicative of their abilities to participate in and contribute to society.

With these findings in mind, the stated purposes of Congress in enacting the Americans With Disabilities Act of 1990 is the following: (1) to provide a clear and comprehensive national mandate for the elimination of discrimination against individuals with disabilities, (2) to provide clear, strong, and consistent enforcement standards, and (3) to insure that the federal government plays a central role in enforcing the standards established by the act on behalf of individuals with disabilities.

The act is meant to protect qualified individuals with disabilities. No employer covered by the act may discriminate against a qualified individual with regard to application procedures, hiring, advancement, discharge, job training, compensation or other terms, conditions or privileges of employment, because of a disability the qualified individual happens to have.

A qualified individual with a disability is defined as an individual with a disability who can, with or without reasonable accommodation, perform the essential functions of the employment position that individual holds or desires. Consideration is to be given to the employer's judgment as to what functions of a particular job are essential. If the employer has prepared a written job description before advertising or interviewing applicants for the job, the written job description is evidence of the essential functions of the job.

Employers may not use job standards, tests, or other selection criteria which screen out or tend to screen out qualified individuals with disabilities, unless the criteria can be shown to be grounded in actual business necessity. Nor may employers select and administer tests which adversely reflect the job-related abilities of those with sensory, speaking, or manual difficulties which impede the test-taking process but which do not detract from the individual's status as a qualified individual for the job in question.

Discrimination against qualified disabled individuals also includes failure to make reasonable accommodation to these individuals' known physical or mental limitations, unless the employer can demonstrate that reasonable accommodation would impose undue hardship. Reasonable accommodation means doing any number of things to assist disabled individuals to adapt to the demands of the workplace. The countervailing consideration to reasonable accommodation is undue hardship. Consistent with reasonable accommodation, to the point where undue hardship is encountered, the employer must make existing facilities used by employees readily accessible to and usable by individuals with disabilities. The employer must also restructure jobs, allow part-time and modified work schedules, acquire new and modify existing equipment, provide qualified readers or interpreters, and adjust or modify training materials and examinations to suit the needs of disabled workers and prospective workers, again only to the point where undue hardship to the employer would take place.

Undue hardship means that the employer will encounter significant difficulty or expense in making reasonable accommodation to the special needs of disabled employees, in relation to the employer's size, overall financial resources, and the number of persons who would benefit.

An employee medical examination may not be conducted, or questions may not be asked during such an examination to discover whether a job applicant or existing employee has a disability or to determine the nature or extent of such a disability, except as related to the examinee's ability to perform job-related functions. An entrance medical examination may be used as a condition of employment only if all applicants are examined similarly with or without regard to the presence of actual or suspected disability.

Records of employee medical examinations must be kept in confidential medical files apart from other employment records. The files can be divulged only to supervisors and managers who need to know about special medical restrictions or to implement reasonable accommodation policies, first aid and safety personnel, and government inspectors investigating compliance with the act.

A drug test is not considered a medical examination for purposes of compliance with the Americans With Disabilities Act of 1990 and the act imposes no restrictions on drug tests. Employees engaging in illegal drug use or suffering from psychoactive substance use disorders resulting from current illegal use of drugs are not considered qualified disabled individuals. In other words, under federal law there is no legal bar to discrimination on the basis of illegal drug use or to holding illegal drug users and alcoholics to the same exacting job-performance standards as everyone else in the workplace. However, individuals who have successfully completed drug rehabilitation, and who are not using drugs illegally, can qualify as disabled persons for purposes of the antidiscrimination provisions of the act. Employers may not discriminate against successfully rehabilitated illegal drug users and addicts on the basis of their former behavior.

Congress has ruled that homosexuality, bisexuality, transvestism, transsexuality, pedophilia, exhibitionism, voyeurism, compulsive gambling, kleptomania, and pyromania are not to be considered disabilities for purposes of the Americans With Disabilities Act of 1990. Thus, there is no barrier imposed by the act to discrimination against individuals who fall within these categories. Although state and local laws may protect one or more of these conditions from employment discrimination, as disabilities or under some other legal rubric.

Enforcement of the Americans with Disabilities Act of 1990 has been vested with the Equal Employment Opportunity Commission. As with other areas of antidiscrimination law, the EEOC has the authority and the continuing duty to issue regulations to define the substance of the law and to set out the procedural framework under which the law will be enforced. Naturally, employers will have to watch the actions of the EEOC very carefully as this new statute is given effect under EEOC substantive guidelines and procedural regulations.

State Laws

As indicated above, every state has its own statute which outlaws discrimination on the basis of disability in employment decisions affecting hiring, compensation, promotions, and other terms and conditions of employment. These state laws apply to most private employers in the state as well as agencies of state and local government. Each state's law is different in how disability is defined, in the remedies offered to individuals who have discrimination claims, and in how those individuals go about presenting their discrimination claims to the appropriate authorities.

State laws differ as to how disabilities are defined. Some states list specific conditions which are protected under the state's anti-discrimination laws. In some of the states which list protected conditions, only conditions specifically noted in the law are protected from employer discrimination. In other states, the list of protected conditions is only meant to illustrate examples of protected conditions and does not preclude other disabling conditions from protection against discrimination. Still other states outlaw disability discrimination in general terms without carefully defining what the terms handicap, disability, or discrimination entail.

Many states have fair employment practices or equal employment opportunity commissions or similar administrative agencies with legal authority to define the terminology used in the state antidiscrimination statute. Where this is the case, it is necessary to obtain and review these regulations carefully before deciding either to file or not to file a complaint concerning possible discriminatory conduct.

Where they are not required to follow specific administrative guidelines, state courts have been very conservative in ruling on disability discrimination claims. They are likely to recognize only relatively serious conditions such as paralysis, blindness, deafness, amputation and congenital degenerative neurological conditions as legally-protected disabilities. They tend to disregard minor injuries, temporary disabling conditions, high blood pressure, psychiatric conditions, alcoholism, and drug addiction as not being within the legal definition of disability.

It may be permissible under state law for an employer to deny employment or advancement to an affected person whose condition makes him or her unable to perform up to the reasonable, objective requirements of a particular job. In fact this is always true in the sense that no employer can be forced to place someone in a job the person just cannot do.

However, in many states and under federal law when applicable, employers must make an effort to find employment that affected persons are able to perform within the organization so that these individuals are given the same chances for financial reward, status, and job satisfaction that nondisabled persons enjoy. In actual practice, balancing the employer's needs and constraints with the disabled employee's rights and aspirations is the most difficult field of controversy in this area of the law.

Barriers to the disabled must be evaluated very carefully to be certain they are based on actual, objective, job-related criteria and are not mere pretexts for discrimination. This is comparatively easy to discern with any particular job, as the job is defined by the employer.

The difficulty is to decide whether the employer can and must modify the stated definition of the job or the physical parameters of the workplace to make them accessible to the disabled worker. Another difficulty is to determine whether the employer's reluctance or refusal to do this is based on permissible considerations having to do with actual hardship or merely represents a pretext for discrimination.

The first court case precedents are not expected under the Americans with Disabilities Act of 1990 until at least two years following the act taking effect in July 1992. However, there are plenty of state court case precedents which serve to define in general how disability discrimination is already being recognized and dealt with under our legal system.

State Court Precedents

One illustrative case decided in 1982 came from the California Supreme Court. It involved a door-to-door insurance salesman denied employment due to high blood pressure which did not impair his ability to do the job in question. The California Fair Employment Practice Commission ruled against the employer. The employer appealed to state superior court, which ruled in favor of the Commission against the employer. The California Supreme Court took the appeal and upheld the Commission and the superior court.

The California Fair Employment Practices Act defined physical "handicap" to include impairment of sight, hearing, speech, or impairment of physical ability because of amputation or loss of function or coordination. However, this did not preclude the Fair Employment Practice Commission from ruling that high blood pressure, which did not adversely affect the ability to do the work in question efficiently, safely, and without danger to health, was also a physical "handicap" which California law would not permit the employer to use as the basis of an adverse employment-related decision.

In ruling against the employer, the commission and the courts were bound to follow the California Fair Employment Practices Act which stated that its provisions were to be liberally construed for the accomplishment of the public policy of the state, and that it is necessary to protect and safeguard the right and opportunity of every person to seek, obtain, and hold employment without discrimination on account of physical disability.

Another interesting case came out of the Supreme Court of Nebraska in 1987. It involved a 24-year-old individual rejected from employment as a junior counselor in a home for orphaned and wayward boys, due to an epileptic condition which had not been symptomatic since age 14. Nebraska law defined a disability protected from employer discriminatory conduct quite explicitly to include epilepsy or seizure disorders unrelated to a person's ability to engage in a particular occupation.

It was relatively easy for the court to recognize that the individual employee in this case was afflicted with a condition protected from employment discrimination under state law, but if and only if he could demonstrate that it did not affect his ability to do his job. Although there had been no seizures in the past ten years, the best medical judgment available was that it was always a possibility he would have a seizure if he forgot his medication, was subjected to unaccustomed levels of stress, or underwent a certain amount of stress and did not adjust his level of medication accordingly.

A large part of the job was transporting youth in vehicles belonging to the home. According to the majority of the court, the safety of the youth could be seriously jeopardized if he were given the job. A dissenting opinion, however, stressed the individual's unblemished medical and work history over the previous ten years. This should have made him eligible for protection from job discrimination by the employer, especially in light of the stated purpose of the Nebraska Fair Employment Practice Act to secure to the disabled full and equal access to employment based on merit and bounded only by the actual disability which an employee or potential employee may be unable to overcome.

Conclusion

These two examples are not by any means exhaustive of the myriad issues which can arise out of controversies in this area, but are only meant to give the reader a taste for the very difficult questions that must usually be answered in these cases. Often a very deserving individual must be denied employment because of factors over which the individual has had absolutely no control. As the dissenting justice in the Nebraska Supreme Court stated, this is, "peculiarly repugnant in a society that prides itself on judging each individual by his or her merits." On the other hand, an employer may be forced to accept an employee whom the employer feels it has very good reasons for refusing to hire or retain. Both examples question our long-held traditions of economic liberty.

Either way there are no easy answers. Nevertheless, employers must try the best they can to become familiar with the applicable laws and to abide by them if they hope to stay out of legal trouble over disability discrimination issues.

Chapter Twelve

Religious Discrimination

Freedom of religion is considered one of the basic civil liberties enjoyed by all Americans. Controversies over conformity versus freedom of religious belief and observance played an important role in the emergence of our federal constitutional system.

Religious discrimination in employment is outlawed by a comprehensive federal legislative and regulatory scheme, and nearly every state has a statute in force which outlaws religious discrimination in employment. Many U.S. states, in fact, have statute laws and case precedents going back much earlier than the Civil Rights Act of 1964, the basic federal statute in this area. State laws generally apply, regardless of the size of the employer or the nature of its operations, and they cover employees of state agencies, county, and local governments as well as employers in the private sector.

State and Federal Law

Since the passage of the Civil Rights Act of 1964, it has been clear under federal law that discrimination on the basis of religious belief and practices is illegal in hiring, benefits, promotions, transfers, employee discipline, or any of the other terms and conditions of employment. The antidiscrimination provisions of the Federal Civil Rights Act of 1964 apply to private and public-sector employers with fifteen or more employees for each working day in each of twenty or more calendar weeks in the current or preceding calendar year. All federal contractors are also subject to the Office of Federal Contract Compliance guidelines on religious and national-origin discrimination. These guidelines went into effect in 1973.

Religion is defined under the law in general terms to include all aspects of religious belief, observance, and practice, which in close cases will not be a very helpful definition at all. Court cases have found that in addition to conventional systems one normally would think of as religious beliefs, atheism is a religion which has the same protected status under the law as Protestantism, Catholicism, Islam, Judaism, and other recognized faiths.

The test for distinguishing religious from political belief systems is the belief in and worship of a Supreme Being. This criterion might seem to preclude the idea of atheism being recognized by the law as a religion, but we have to remember that in the early history of our country, freedom from having to follow another's religion or to have no religion at all was as much a part of religious liberty as the freedom to practice one's own faith.

The controversial cases have been when the courts have had to distinguish certain religious beliefs, which are protected from discrimination, from political ideologies, which are not. Membership in the Black Muslim faith is a religion, while membership in the Ku Klux Klan is not. Except for the KKK, employers have to give their employees the benefit of the doubt when employees claim that their individual beliefs and perhaps odd or idiosyncratic practices are, in fact, religions, assuming these beliefs and practices are not of a purely political character.

Cases of blatant religious discrimination in hiring and promotions are becoming rare, due to a general raising of consciousness in our society over the pernicious effects of all forms of discrimination. In addition, there is an increasing willingness of victims to use state and federal fair employment agencies and civil courts to obtain redress of discriminatory policies and practices.

Much of the litigation these agencies and our courts have seen recently in the area of religious discrimination involves employees with alternative Sabbath observances, special religious holidays or holy days, different standards of personal appearance, and other individual religious practices and observances which may or may not require special concessions from their employers.

Moslems, members of nontraditional Christian denominations and Jews are suing their employers over these issues on grounds of religious discrimination. Because of this fact, employers in many instances now have to carefully accommodate employees with special religious needs, when that is possible, rather than face the expense and embarrassment of discrimination litigation.

On the other hand, employers need not under all conceivable circumstances give their employees the upper hand every time religion is raised as the basis for conduct which does not comport with reasonable employment policies. The key to understanding employers' responsibilities and rights in this area is knowing where the line is drawn between reasonable accommodation and business necessity and employer hardship.

Reasonable Accommodation

Federal and state laws require reasonable accommodation to employees' religious needs, and failure to make reasonable accommodation amounts to religious discrimination. This does not mean that employees are automatically entitled to any days off they choose, to bow out of certain job requirements on religious grounds, to disrupt the workplace with religious observances or religious proselytizing, or to adopt the particular standards of dress and personal grooming which their religions demands, contrary to employer standards.

Much depends on the hardship the employer will experience if employees' differing religious needs are fully met. Employers who can realistically do so must let employees have the day or part of the day off for religious reasons, or reschedule other employees in place of employees who have different Sabbaths when they must not work or who must not work on Sundays. But if this is not economically feasible, given the size and nature of the employer's operations, it is not necessary to accommodate employees in this way just to avoid charges of religious discrimination.

The basic requirement of reasonable accommodation under the law must yield to consideration of the fact that conflict will generally ensue among employees when some employees try to claim religion as grounds for preferential consideration over other employees for the days they want to be off work. Many employees will want Friday evenings, Saturdays, or Sundays off, and not necessarily because their religions forbid them to work on these days. Rules of seniority are a permitted basis for allowing a senior employee to take the day off for personal reasons, while a junior employee with less seniority is forced to work despite a clear religious dictate to the contrary. One employee cannot always use religion to get what he or she wants at the expense of others who want the same things but do not express their needs or desires on religious grounds.

Balancing Work Schedules with Religious Holidays

When the employer's operations do require Friday, Saturday, or Sunday work, and no one is available or wishes to cover for an employee who needs the day off to observe the Sabbath, and it is just not economically feasible to hire additional employees just for this reason, an employee can be required either to work or to consider looking for a more amenable situation somewhere else. Days off have to be apportioned on the basis of fairness to everyone, and one employee cannot have the day off simply because it is his or her Sabbath or a religious holiday or holy day, in preference to another employee who also wants the same day off.

Employers are also required to be cognizant of whether scheduling pre-employment interviews, testing, or medical exams conflicts with certain minorities Sabbath's or other special days and restricts their free access to the job market. Employers must demonstrate that they would suffer from undue hardship or that there is an overriding business necessity in scheduling pre-employment activities to conflict with potential employees' religious observances.

Another important issue is that as a general rule, employees who seek preferential treatment on religious grounds must be prepared to demonstrate the sincerity of their beliefs. It is difficult for a court or administrative agency to step inside the mind of an employee complaining of religious discrimination or anyone else for that matter, but as a practical matter employees have lost religious-discrimination cases where they have been guilty of a history of inconsistent approach to the religious practices for which they have sought protection under the law.

For example, an employee who allegedly cannot work on the Sabbath or on certain other days cannot use his or her religion selectively to get out of work on some days while working on other days which are equally proscribed by his or her religion. An employee who professes adherence to a certain faith, but takes it upon himself or herself to decide which of the faith's holy days to observe and which to go about business as usual, will be subject to charges of insincerity. The ulterior motivation may be obvious for an employee who picks which days to work and which days to be off for alleged religious reasons, but for legal purposes the correct framing of the issue is that the employee's beliefs are not sincere and, therefore, are not entitled to protection on grounds of religious discrimination.

In defining the holidays for which employers will grant leave, it bears notice that our courts, for better or for worse, have ruled that Christmas and Easter have acquired secondary secular meanings in American society apart from their religious significance to members of most Christian faiths. These days stand on a different footing than Rosh Hashanah, Passover, and special days observed by Moslems and other American religious minorities. It is not discriminatory to treat Christmas and Easter differently than the special holidays or holy days of other faiths.

Norms for Dress and Grooming

Aside from the issues surrounding balancing work schedules with different Sabbaths and special religious observances, employers should be aware that they are allowed to enforce realistic norms for dress and grooming, despite the fact that this will curtail certain employees' from wearing special religious costumes or growing and wearing their hair and beards for religious reasons in ways out of step with the grooming standards of the mainstream of contemporary society. The important consideration here is that there must be some objective reason behind employers requiring employees to maintain certain standards of appearance. Otherwise, employers open themselves to accusations that they have exercised their discretion over employees in these matters on discriminatory grounds.

Employees who do not routinely deal with the public are often much looser with their appearances than employees who must uphold a certain public image considered proper for the organization. If some employees can come to work dirty, dishevelled, groomed as skinheads, bikers, or punk rockers, that is, groomed or dressed in one or more ways considered unusual or even repulsive by conventional contemporary standards, other employees should be allowed to wear turbans, yarmulkes, long hair, beards, or unusual religious costumes. If there is a double standard in this context, religious discrimination is the only logical explanation a human rights agency or civil court will likely be able to discern.

There is nothing wrong with dress and appearance codes, as long as the employer's standards bear some realistic relationship to the employer's public image and are not a mere pretext for discrimination directed at religious minorities, and as long as appearance standards are not applied in a discriminatory fashion against employees who desire to express their religious identifications publicly.

The employer can expect professional people to dress and groom themselves according to accepted professional standards in the community, that is, to wear suits and have "normal" haircuts and facial hair. Retail and other customer service personnel can be required to maintain their appearances in line with accepted community standards, even when those community standards are admittedly somewhat intolerant of individual differences, style, religious, and ethnic preference.

Religious Proselytizing

Religious proselytizing on the job can be regulated or forbidden by employers outright, but this must be done in a uniform fashion which affects all faiths equally. No matter how important it is to certain employees to spread the messages of their faiths and to convert unbelievers, there is no secular authority prohibiting employers from curtailing unwanted behavior of this nature in the workplace.

The same is true with daily prayers, meditation, chanting, and scriptural readings which interfere with the normal conduct of the employers' operations. Employers do not have to allow employees to interfere with others, disrupt the ordinary flow of operations to say their prayers, meditate, or engage in other ritual religious conduct on the job. On the other hand, if employers do choose to allow certain conduct of this nature, they must realistically allow all conduct of this nature, without regard to their own personal feelings about the validity of others' beliefs of the appropriateness of their religious practices.

The courts have in some cases permitted distribution of religious leaflets in malls and shopping centers, despite the fact that these places are technically private property, because these places are held open to the public as public places and because there are no comparable truly public places in many localities where diverging viewpoints can be aired freely. However, offices and factories are not public places. Employees of retail businesses are there as employees, not as customers, and as far as they are concerned, they are on private property where the employer's rules govern their behavior.

It should be apparent that it is probably more feasible for the employer to keep all overt expressions of religion out of the workplace rather than to risk bias charges by allowing one faith to practice its observances and forbidding this luxury to others.

Employers also must be very circumspect about forcing, encouraging, or tacitly permitting their own faiths' religious practices in the workplace. This will no doubt offend certain potentially litigious employees, even those who have no particular desire to engage in their own alternative observances, but would rather keep the subject of religion out of their daily work lives, as is their clear prerogative under federal and state antidiscrimination law.

There are two sides to this issue, and employers cannot themselves use the workplace to spread their own religious ideas, despite their feeling about their own religious freedom and their right to engage in any activity of their choosing on their own premises. And they certainly cannot require or expect employees to engage in religious or devotional activities of the employer's choosing, either during or outside of working hours.

Although it will not affect the majority of employers, it is worth noting that religious educational institutions are exempt from the federal EEOC regulations covering religious discrimination in employment. These institutions are free to discriminate with respect to religion in hiring employees for any and all positions.

Conclusion

Religious discrimination is one area where employers do have certain prerogatives in maintaining the orderly flow of their operations in the face of employees' desires to practice their religions on the job. But where there is no adverse impact on operations or none to which reasonable accommodation cannot be made, religion must be allowed its expression in the workplace. The most important consideration is impartiality to every religious faith and every system of religious belief which could claim protection under the law. Seniority must be the guide to decisions governing religious preferences for days off. Of course, no religious preference in hiring, compensation, or other terms and conditions of employment is likely to survive scrutiny by the courts or fair employment agencies.

Chapter Thirteen

Race Discrimination

Race discrimination is a subject with a long and bitterly-fought historical development in the United States. The first legislative efforts on the national level go back to the Civil Rights Act of 1871, enacted shortly after the end of the Civil War to deal with the plight of the newly-freed black slaves.

Shortly after the end of the Civil War, the Thirteenth, Fourteenth, and Fifteenth Amendments to the U.S. Constitution were enacted, again primarily to attempt to insure legal respect for the civil rights of the newly-freed slaves. These amendments have been given an interpretation by the courts which now extends far beyond the area of race relations and have come to represent essential cornerstones of the civil rights of all persons in the United States.

Throughout the period since the Civil War, particularly during the Jim Crow years from about 1890 until World War II was in progress, our national commitment to the cause of racial equality admittedly was not as strong as it could and should have been. But since the ground-breaking school desegregation rulings of the Supreme Court in the late 1950s and the inception of the civil rights movement shortly thereafter, our national consciousness has definitely swung solidly in favor of full racial equality, at least as an officially-stated fundamental American social value.

In light of our history, it is difficult to understate the importance of the strong commitment of the legislative, executive, and judicial branches of government on the federal, state, and local levels to the cause of full racial equality, not only in employment but in housing, transportation, education, voting rights, and almost every facet of our national life. Even without governmental compulsion, almost every segment of society is now publicly committed to racial equality and will officially look down upon any vestige of racial segregation or inequality with profound displeasure. Any employer not fully on the side of full racial equality in employment must realize that serious legal trouble is surely inevitable.

State and Federal Law

Racial discrimination is now outlawed by Title VII of the Civil Rights Act of 1964, which applies across the board to all employers who have fifteen or more employees in each of twenty or more calendar weeks in the current or preceding calendar year. On the federal level, every agency which does business with private sector employers or provides funding in one way or another to the public or private-sectors requires that recipients of federal funding be free from racial bias in employment decisions. Each federal agency has its own regulations on the subject, which all boil down to the essential point that race discrimination is strictly forbidden. Larger employers, in fact, have also been required at times to demonstrate a firm commitment to affirmative action along racial lines in order to continue to receive federal money.

Every state also outlaws racial discrimination in private and public sector employment. Each state's laws are different and must be consulted separately by employers in each state, but employers are generally safe in assuming that state law makes no distinctions over the size of an employer, the number of employees, or the nature of the employer's operations where racial equality of employment opportunity are concerned. Actually, many of the states have race discrimination laws on their books which predate the Federal Civil Rights Act of 1964, which have and perhaps have not been fully enforced at various times in the state's history.

It should be obvious that any sort of overt discrimination against racial minorities or individual minority-group members will be highly suspect if the matter is brought before an administrative agency such as the Equal Employment Opportunity Commission, a state fair employment commission, or a state or federal court. The employer is technically not presumed innocent where racial bias is the charge. Where a minority group member or members, or someone espousing their cause, can show simply that a single member or a racial minority as a group have been treated adversely, or even differently than nonminorities, the employer will have the burden of justifying its conduct on nondiscriminatory grounds. And justifying any conduct which classifies, separates, segregates, or treats racial minorities differently than others is virtually an impossible task.

The Civil Rights Act of 1871 and many state antibias statutes were theoretically the law of the land throughout the Jim Crow period. Despite the fact that well-intentioned laws have been on the books for some time, racism of one sort or another is still rife in our society. It is now recognized that even enlightened, well-intentioned individuals still suffer from subtle unconscious prejudices against racial minorities which will color their thinking and influence their actions to these minorities' detriment. For this reason it is necessary for the law to categorically eradicate racial distinctions of every sort, without regard for justifications offered in their defense, no matter how innocent, plausible, or artfully conceived they may be. Every form of justification in this area will be seen under the law only as a rationalization for illegal behavior.

Whenever a racial minority member is treated adversely in the employment arena, charges of racial bias can be expected. Every racial distinction is presumed by the law to be motivated by prejudice. If conscientious business owners, managers, executives, supervisors, and human resources and personnel professionals are willing to undertake a certain amount of effort and risk a certain amount of embarrassment, they can discover the reasons for the law's deep wisdom in this area. Although it is not as fashionable now as it was perhaps in the late 1960s or early 1970s, members of different racial groups can always do more to explore their perceptions, attitudes, and feelings toward one another. If they take the time to do so, they will likely find that old-fashioned prejudices, stereotypes, and even fears are not as long-gone as everyone would like to believe. It is this kind of consciousness-raising on the psychological, interpersonal, and social levels that can do a great deal toward educating individuals about their own internal psychic makeups, ingrained patterns of racial perception, and social interaction. These can play a largely underrated role in generating legal trouble for the organization over racial-bias issues.

Requirements of the Law

The overall approach of the law is not to wait for individual acts to take place or for individual victims of real or imagined discrimination to come forward. The law requires employers to keep elaborate records of employment decisions affecting employees along with their racial characteristics, in order for the EEOC to ascertain that racial bias is not occurring. This requirement, for administrative reasons, applies only to employers with 100 or more employees, who must file annually an Employer Information Report EEO-1, known also as Standard Form 100. Fulfilling this requirement virtually necessitates having professional human resources professionals on board or available on a consulting basis who are familiar with equal employment opportunity law and able to assist the employer with its legal duties in this regard.

Based on the information filed with the authorities, the EEOC is able to take action against employers whose organizational racial makeups suggest that discrimination is taking place, even if that discrimination shows itself only in disparate impact of employment decisions on minority groups rather than more overt manifestations of bias which might lead specific individuals to file complaints. And if charges are filed, past informational filings with the EEOC can be examined to determine whether there is a basis for charges of systematic bias based on disparate impact of employment decisions on minorities in the particular workplace then coming under scrutiny.

Disparate impact analysis has been a major factor in sex discrimination litigation and is discussed in Chapter 14. Generally, disparate impact refers to subtle or institutional biases which do not provoke individual incidents, but which become manifest only when the percentages of minorities versus nonminorities in desirable or more sought-after positions is out of line with the percentages which have been determined to be appropriate for the makeup of the population of the workplace.

Affirmative action is the general remedy where disparate impact is found to affect minorities adversely. Affirmative action is a policy of aiding minorities in one fashion or another to move into more prestigious, better-paying, or otherwise more desirable jobs in order to rectify the percentage imbalances of minorities in such positions within the organization. Affirmative action is also discussed in more detail in Chapter 14.

Smaller employers are not absolutely required by the EEOC to keep records of hiring, promotions, compensation, layoffs, discipline, and termination of employees along with the employee's racial characteristics, which could be reconstructed at some point to show how the company is or is not effectively dealing with problems which could surface over issues of racial bias. But if employers are committed to the cause, at least for no other reason than to minimize their legal exposure to racial-discrimination litigation, they are permitted to keep such records and to classify employees along racial grounds for purposes of monitoring their own efforts at human-rights compliance.

Employers cannot be educated too forcefully about the importance of keeping accurate, detailed, and objective records of all aspects of employee job performance. This suggestion is stressed throughout this book. After a bias charge is made, or a wrongful discharge suit is filed, it is too late to reconstruct an individual's employment history. There may or may not be perfectly legitimate reasons for discharging or taking other adverse action against a minority group member, but without careful, objective documentation of that individual's work history before the fact, the employer will be wide open to substantial exposure on grounds of racial discrimination.

Larger and smaller employers alike must also be aware that there are extremely elaborate regulations promulgated by the EEOC dealing with the subject of employee selection procedures. Basically what these guidelines deal with are pencil-and-paper tests given to prospective employees and existing employees being evaluated for vertical movement within the company or entry into job-training programs.

Understanding the concerns minorities and those sensitive to their problems have with pencil-and-paper tests again requires a short excursion back into the history of race relations in the United States. For a considerable period of time after the Civil War, even as late as the 1960s, blacks were not expressly disenfranchised by local and state law, but were effectively prevented from voting, aside from overt intimidation, by patterns of legal chicanery in which voter literacy tests played no small part. These voter literacy tests, scored by prejudiced white officials, were impossible for blacks to pass, no matter how intelligent, educated, literate, and competent they were to vote. They offered a seemingly plausible rationalization for most blacks' legal ineligibility for placement on the registered voting rolls.

Seemingly legitimate educational distinctions in our society often turn on social class considerations, and social class considerations often bespeak underlying racial differences. Selection processes based on education, apart from specific attributes essential to the job, can easily become a subtle excuse for racism. Even at the present time, pencil-and-paper tests such as college and professional school entrance exams are under assault as biased in favor of persons from Caucasian or more affluent social-class backgrounds. These tests are attacked as tending to allow certain groups to demonstrate higher test scores without any particular direct correlation with later professional success. This is apart from the fact that the people who score higher also happen to have been born into more advantaged racial and social-class backgrounds in the first place.

The EEOC's Uniform Guidelines on Employee Selection Procedures strongly suggest that employers, regardless of size, who want to use any sort of pencil-and-paper test to evaluate employees do so only with professional assistance from in-house or outside people. These people must be familiar with the process of qualifying such tests for unbiased use under the EEOC Uniform Guidelines and with the proper procedures for administering and grading such tests in an unbiased manner. Administration and use of pencil-and-paper tests and understanding the complex Uniform Guidelines are not subjects for amateurs. Employers who do not wish to obtain competent professional assistance here should simply not venture into this area.

As a further general consideration, employers should also be cognizant that many contemporary race discrimination cases involve persons who are members of more than one minority group, who are asserting rights under more than one recognized rubric of antidiscrimination law, perhaps arising out of separate incidents of illegal employer conduct. Examples of this phenomenon might be a disabled black man or pregnant married black woman who claim to have been the victims of perhaps many prejudiced employment decisions which are alleged to have offended the law in different particulars.

These cases are quite common, more common than most employers may want to think, and have to be sorted out by treating each set of allegations separately according to the principles which govern each particular area of antidiscrimination law. An employee or prospective employee who is able to allege and prove more than one ground for discriminatory treatment is generally only entitled to what he or she has lost or been denied because of any particular act of discrimination. The fact that the particular act involved more than one form of discrimination concomitantly does not increase the employer's exposure beyond compensating the disaffected individual for what he or she has lost.

An employee denied a promotion due to disability discrimination who successfully goes before an administrative agency or civil court will be entitled to the promotion, with back pay and benefits to the date when the promotion should have been forthcoming. The fact that the employee was denied the same promotion due to race, marital status, and disability discrimination will not augment the employee's remedy or enlarge the employer's exposure, except possibly where punitive damages are an issue. But an employee who has suffered different acts of discrimination on the same or different grounds is entitled to recompense for each act as if each act were a separate case. There are even cases where a prior act serves to augment the effect of a later act of discrimination. For example, an employee who is passed over for promotion once on racial grounds and then is passed over again when individuals from among those previously promoted are themselves promoted to even higher levels within the organization.

Conclusion

A sober consideration of the possibilities should convince all rational employers, managers, executives, and human resources people to become as firmly committed to the cause of racial equality as the rest of our society is.

Chapter Fourteen

Sex Discrimination

Sex discrimination refers to the process of treating women employees and prospective employees differently because of their gender. This general subject has been divided into several chapters in this book because there are individual topics in the area of sex discrimination which merit special attention. The present chapter deals with general considerations in gender-based employment discrimination, while other chapters have been included dealing separately with sexual harassment, pregnancy discrimination, and marital status discrimination. All of these issues fall under the very general legal rubric of sex or gender-based discrimination.

Pregnancy and marital status discrimination are complex subjects, but they require little introduction to alert the reader as to what in general terms they entail. For readers who are unfamiliar with the terminology used in the field of antidiscrimination law, sexual harassment refers to the practice of employers exploiting female employees for sexual purposes and the practice of engaging in intimidating, offensive, or hostile conduct of a sexual nature in the workplace likewise directed at female employees.

In certain places in this book sex discrimination is referred to as gender-based discrimination in order to remove any confusion with sexual harassment. Although sexual harassment is considered one very individualized form of sex or gender-based discrimination, there is much more to the subject than that.

Sex discrimination is outlawed by Title VII of the Civil Rights Act of 1964, the basic federal statute against employment discrimination. Title VII applies to all employers with fifteen or more employees in each of twenty or more calendar weeks in the current or immediately preceding calendar year.

Most states' fair employment practices statutes also outlaw sex discrimination as well as sexual harassment, but some of the states have not gone as far as the federal government where pregnancy and marital status discrimination are concerned. Employers must also check to see whether their local municipalities have ordinances on the subject of sex discrimination. As a general rule, state and local laws do not exempt employers based on the number of employees they have, so that every employer must assume that some law somewhere will prevent sex discrimination in employment.

Laws of Sex Discrimination

To comprehend how the laws operate in the area of sex discrimination, it is useful to review and to understand the reasons behind them. One of the stated purposes of the laws in this area is to keep employers from making employment decisions based on general assumptions concerning the employment characteristics of women compared with men. Some of these impermissible assumptions are that women may be treated less than equally with men because they have a higher turnover rate than men due to a number of different assumptions. These include family considerations competing with work-related factors, emotional instability, or other grossly stereotyped suppositions which have traditionally separated men and women where hiring and job opportunities were at stake. These stereotypes may have included the idea that women were more suited than men to certain tasks such as assembly of intricate manufactured articles or to routine clerical work, while men were better at complex, nonroutine jobs requiring special levels of gender-dependent mechanical insight or managerial aptitudes which women were not felt to possess. Men were at one time also felt to excel in employment activities requiring organization, initiative and aggressiveness, while women were better left to domestic responsibilities, cooking, and nurturing.

In fact, laws in many states, which were considered very enlightened by late nineteenth and early twentieth-century standards, actually forbade the employment of women in industrial occupations considered too arduous or dangerous for them. These laws also gave women special consideration in terms of mandatory rest and meal periods and restricted the hours women could work, both the number of hours per day and what specific hours of the day women were permitted in the workplace.

What was considered progressive during the age of women's suffrage came to be looked down upon as patronizing toward women, and thus discriminatory, with the advent of more contemporary concerns over equal rights.

Title VII of the Civil Rights Act of 1964 effectively put an end to these laws inasmuch as they gave preferential treatment to women. The Equal Employment Opportunity Commission has tried with its guidelines on sex discrimination to finesse the application of these laws rather than to overrule them outright, by requiring employers to give men the same treatment as women are required to receive under state law, and by making it discriminatory to refuse to employ women to avoid having to give them the special treatment state law may require.

If there is no reasonable way for employers to treat men and women the same and still abide by state laws designed to foster special treatment for women industrial workers, the employer must disregard state law and consider it to have been overruled by Title VII. The employer must then treat men and women equally by giving neither the benefit of the special consideration mandated by these old state laws.

Expressions of Gender-Based Discrimination

The laws against sex discrimination prohibit many overt expressions of gender-based discrimination. One of these is the maintenance of "male" and "female" job classifications or maintenance of separate male and female seniority systems. All jobs must be open to all qualified applicants, regardless of gender, and all employees must be treated alike with respect to seniority.

One of the outmoded prejudices meant to be rectified by the laws against sex discrimination is that women belong in the home rather than in the workplace, or that men's primary sphere of activity is work while women are meant to concentrate on child bearing, child rearing, and family life. Thus, it is against the spirit as well as the letter of the law against sex discrimination to expect that women will step aside to allow men to be promoted or to keep their jobs in times of force reductions, as if work were more important or more appropriate for men than for women.

Since it is illegal to engage in such overt discrimination in actual practices relative to hiring, seniority, and promotions, it is likewise illegal to advertise or to list employment opportunities with so much as any hint that the employer will be using any gender-based preference in selecting among available job applicants. The once widespread practice of advertising in "Help Wanted - Male" and "Help Wanted - Female" classified columns is strictly verboten, as is any other more subtle form of gender-based employment advertising. In fact, in preparing job applications and conducting all pre-employment inquiries, the employer cannot give any indication that there will be any hiring preference with regard to the gender of the applicant. Overt discrimination against women is illegal, despite the insistence some employers have advanced in defense of discrimination that they were only acting out of concern for the preferences of coworkers, customers, or clients in dealing with an all-male work force or in dealing with only males in certain occupations. None of these is a valid reason for employers maintaining policies or engaging in practices of sex discrimination in hiring, job assignments, or promotions.

Fringe benefits are another area where employers are not allowed to discriminate on the basis of employees' gender. Fringe benefits include medical, hospital, accident and life insurance, retirement benefits, profit sharing, bonuses, and sick, annual and personal leave policies.

Benefits

Benefits such as medical or disability insurance which are available only to a "head of household" or "principal wage earner" have been found to be largely a pretext for discrimination against women. Whether or not one is the head of a household or principal wage earner relates to one's personal living or family arrangements and has nothing whatsoever to do with performance on the job. Forms or employment compensation which have hinged on arrangements of this nature have traditionally discriminated against women, and are not permissible under the EEOC guidelines against sex discrimination.

It is also a carry-over from outdated prejudiced ways of thinking to provide benefits to the wives of male workers but not to the husbands of females. Even more offensive would be the now illegal practice of affording maternity benefits to wives of male workers but not to female employees, which runs afoul of the law either from the perspective of sex discrimination or pregnancy discrimination. And, conversely, under federal case law, wives of male employees are entitled to the same pregnancy-related benefits as female employees must receive. It makes no difference as far as required compliance with Title VII is concerned that it might be more costly to provide benefits to one sex rather than the other or to the spouses of one sex rather than spouses of the other. Men and women must be treated alike.

Determining Whether Sex Discrimination Exists

Some consideration should be given in this discussion to how the EEOC, state fair employment agencies, and the federal and state courts go about determining whether sex discrimination exists or has taken place with respect to a particular employer.

The EEOC guidelines and state laws have set out certain practices which are discriminatory on their face, such as restricting ads, notices, listings, or effective consideration for employment in certain jobs only to men or only to women. Another facially discriminatory policy might be restricting benefits to families of male employees or reserving certain job "perks" to men only. In these cases the employee or employees aggrieved by the employer's conduct will be able to make out a case of sex discrimination rather easily. This will require the administrative agency hearing the bias charge to force the employer to change its ways and to make up for past conduct, unless the employer can show a bona fide occupational qualification for its conduct.

Bona Fide Occupational Qualifications

A bona fide, or good faith, occupational qualification for facially discriminatory conduct is the way out that employers accused of discrimination always have, at least on paper. In actual practice, however, a bona fide occupational qualification is rarely, if ever, sustained. Even if the employer succeeds in the unlikely endeavor of proving a bona fide occupational qualification, the disaffected employee or employees can always come back and try to demonstrate that the alleged bona fide occupational qualification is a mere pretext for discrimination.

Disparate Impact Analysis

Where disaffected minority employees are not able to prove the employer has done something discriminatory on its face, but want to establish the existence of more subtle layers of discrimination within the organizational makeup, the employees and their counsel must resort to disparate impact analysis. Disparate impact analysis is a specialty within the field of employment law. It involves comparing the incidence of certain factors, possibly indicative of discrimination in the particular employer's workplace, under scrutiny with established norms for industry and the economy at large.

For example, it may be that experts in the field can show that no more than a certain percentage of women employees in a manufacturing concern should have clerical jobs paying less than union scale for semi-skilled factory operatives, or, conversely, that no more than a certain percentage of the clerical people should be women. Or perhaps a certain percentage of women employees should be supervisors, and no more than a certain percentage of the total number of supervisors should be men. If the first percentage is too high, and the second is too low compared to established national norms, it is likely that the employer is or has been engaging in some sort of discrimination along the lines which have traditionally segregated women into certain jobs and restricted their advancement to more important, better-paying and more responsible positions.

Even if no one is able to find facially discriminatory practices which would obviously tend to restrict employment opportunities for women, if the disparate-impact data do not compute properly, there is likely some sort of discrimination going on, which may well need to be corrected.

Where identified aggrieved parties have been able to prove they have been the victims of facially discriminatory employer conduct, they are the ones entitled to reinstatement, advancement, and awards of back-pay and benefits to remedy what has been done to them individually or as an identified group. However, where women as a class have been treated in a disparate fashion, the remedy is usually some sort of affirmative action program to bring the relevant percentages in line with accepted norms, leaving open the question of which actual women will benefit from a certain amount of remedial consideration and which will not.

Bringing such a program on-line is usually accomplished either by voluntary employer conduct or by conciliatory cooperation between the employer and the EEOC or appropriate state fair employment practices agency. Where employers have been recalcitrant at cooperating with administrative agencies over these issues, the agencies have been able to enlist the full support of the federal and state courts, which are able to levy fines and contempt citations against individuals and corporations which refuse to cooperate. Employers are as entitled to their day in court as anyone, but in matters of employment discrimination the courts almost always uphold the EEOC and appropriate state agencies, except where the agency can be shown to have acted arbitrarily or in clear violation of law. In matters of independent fact-finding and exercise of judgment with respect to appropriateness of specific remedies, administrative antidiscrimination agencies will almost always prevail.

Other than where required to do so by administrative agencies or the courts, employers are able under some circumstances to undertake voluntary affirmative action programs. The problem with these programs, despite their laudatory stated aims, is that they can operate to discriminate in reverse fashion against members of what is considered the majority.

Affirmative Action

Affirmative action is still very controversial. It continues to receive a good deal of attention in the federal courts, on Capitol Hill, and in state court and assembly chambers. The problem is to balance the rights of the majority to equal treatment with the rights of minority members who belong to minority groups traditionally victimized by discrimination. The greater the degree to which the specific persons who represent the affected minority group in the particular organization in question have actually been victimized by past discrimination at the hands of the particular organization, the more likely is that organization's affirmative action plan to pass muster against charges of reverse discrimination.

On the other hand, where affirmative action is used as a tool to restructure society in general along more egalitarian lines, without regard to the participation of the affected majority in a particular setting in acts of discrimination directed at the affected minority in the same setting, it is reasonably likely that affirmative action in the particular context under consideration will not stand up.

Organizations which intend to engage in affirmative action should only do so after realistic appraisal of their own history of discriminatory conduct. An affirmative action plan should be tailored to deal only with what the organization has done in the past or is doing currently, rather than being concerned with considerations of equity and justice which transcend its own limited boundaries.

Whether or not one agrees with affirmative action, it may be necessary to remedy past injustices perpetrated by overt acts of discrimination or policies and practices which have resulted in disparate impact on minority groups. Likewise, whether or not one agrees with it, affirmative action cannot go beyond that.

Many employers have found a limited position to be effective in dealing with the strongly conflicting considerations on both sides of the arguments over affirmative action, which may represent a compromise between doing nothing and doing too much or going too far. That position is one which seeks to help employees and prospective employees who happen to be disadvantaged in some fashion or happen to be members of minority groups to compete with men and other majority groups on the same standards, rather than selectively relaxing standards or having to make employment decisions blatantly on the basis of reversely-discriminatory grounds. However, there really are no easy answers to the questions raised by affirmative action.

Conclusion

Before coming to any real conclusions concerning the law of gender discrimination, it is necessary to proceed further into the complex material which follows. Overt discrimination on gender-based grounds is receding. But sexual harassment, pregnancy, and marital status discrimination, where the rules are less clearly understood by nonlawyers, are still very fruitful areas for litigation. Every employer needs to make the effort to understand the law and to apply it in formulating sound policies.

Chapter Fifteen

Sexual Harassment

Laws against sexual harassment on the job have been the basis for a large portion of the employment-related human rights litigation since the early 1970s. It is difficult to quantify the number of sexual harassment cases seen by state courts, state fair employment commissions, the EEOC, and the federal courts, since only a relatively few cases which actually break new legal ground are reported publicly and come to the attention of legal commentators. And it is almost impossible to quantify the number of complaints being resolved informally between employers and disaffected employees, because it is usually a feature of settlement agreements that the fact of settlement and the underlying situation which led to the complaint not be disclosed publicly.

Nevertheless, after a major upsurge in administrative complaints and litigation in state and federal court in the 1970s, the volume of legal proceedings being fought over issues involving sexual harassment on the job seems to be on the decline. Employers are finally becoming cognizant of their legal duties in this area and the substantial direct financial costs in store for them in compensating victims who are willing to present their cases through proper legal channels. Employers should also be aware of the public embarrassment and drain on organizational morale and efficiency which usu-

ally comes when the company is on the losing end of an emotionally highly-charged legal ordeal.

Employers, like all facets of society, are participating in a growing change in consciousness about the roles of men and women in
general and, more specifically, the roles of men and women who
happen to be employers, managers and supervisors, and employees
in the same enterprises. The law is continually redefining the rights
of employees in the workplace, and the prevalent trend is definitely
toward an upgrading of employees' rights as far as the degree of
dignity and respect owed to them by their employers is concerned.

State and Federal Law

Sexual harassment is outlawed by federal law, under Title VII of the
Civil Rights Act of 1964, the basic federal antidiscrimination statute.
The EEOC has promulgated regulations which define illegal sexual
harassment and impose the affirmative duty on employers to prevent its occurrence. The EEOC guidelines on sexual harassment are
found in the Code of Federal Regulations, Title 29, Section 1604.11.
State laws against gender-based discrimination also have been construed in one way or another to outlaw sexual harassment.

Title VII and the EEOC guidelines apply only to private and
public employers with fifteen or more employees for each working
day in twenty or more calendar weeks during the current or immediately preceding calendar year. State laws generally apply to all
employers in the state, including state and local governments.

Originally, both state and federal civil rights legislation only expressly forbade gender-based employment discrimination, along
with discrimination based on race, religion, national origin, and
certain other factors. The EEOC, state fair employment opportunity
agencies, and state and federal courts, on the other hand, recognized right away that sexual harassment was one of the specific
unlawful behavior patterns which gender-based antidiscrimination
laws were meant to rectify.

This was similar to the manner in which it was recognized that
marital status discrimination and pregnancy discrimination fell
under the overall rubric of gender-based discrimination which the

laws were seeking to eradicate. Discriminatory practices of not opening certain jobs to women or paying women less than men for the same work was originally what came to mind when gender-based discrimination was first mentioned.

Sexual Harassment Defined

Sexual harassment, as defined under federal and state law, whether that law is found in explicit legislative or administrative enactments or the more elusive case law drawn from court precedents, falls basically into two conceptually distinct forms of wrongful conduct. One form of sexual harassment occurs when undergoing unwelcome sexual advances or unwelcome requests for sexual favors becomes either explicitly or implicitly a term or condition of an individual's employment such that submission to or rejection of such conduct is used by the employer as the basis for employment decisions affecting the individual. The other form sexual harassment can take is where conduct of a sexual nature on the job creates a work environment so intimidating, hostile, or offensive that it seriously affects the individual's psychological well-being.

It is possible for these two conceptual distinctions to overlap in any individual case, but that is not necessary for sexual harassment to take place. For example, where a supervisor insists that a subordinate sleep with him in order to get a raise in salary or a different shift assignment, it is possible that the individual will be able to demonstrate that the supervisor's actions have created an intimidating, hostile, or offensive work environment. However, sexual harassment takes place under circumstances where sex is made a term or condition of employment even if the individual is not able to show that the work environment has become intimidating, hostile, or offensive. In some instances an individual may be unable to demonstrate that any serious adverse psychological consequences affecting his or her well-being have taken place.

On the other hand, the individual may be the victim of sexual harassment even though there may be nothing of a sexual nature expected of the individual in exchange for more advantageous treatment by supervisors or management. This may occur where an individual is subject to such things as offensive sexual jokes, embarrassing sexual innuendo, or sexual propositions meant to bother, upset, or intimidate the person rather than actually to get the individual into bed.

Regardless of which type of sexual harassment takes place, the more severe the adverse consequences which the individual can demonstrate, the more the individual will stand to receive as compensation. While one individual might just say "no" to a supervisor's first round of advances, walk out, retain counsel, and sue successfully for the promotion or whatever he or she has been denied by his or her refusal, without undergoing a great deal of emotional damage in the process, another might conceivably endure a long pattern of abuse or intimidation to the point of psychological collapse. That individual may become entitled to a vastly different measure of compensation.

Obligations of Employers

Employers, managers, and supervisors should be aware that the damages awarded where the employee is successful with a sexual harassment claim can be very substantial. On the other hand, there are many cases which will not prove to be successful. Management does not have to treat every instance where sexuality is demonstrated or sexual feelings are expressed in the workplace as a potentially disastrous legal nightmare waiting to happen. It is important to learn to recognize the boundaries between what administrative agencies and the courts will and will not recognize as actionable so that effective risk-management procedures can be implemented.

It should be apparent that the first major type of behavior defined as sexual harassment can only occur between an employee and someone higher up in the company hierarchy or with someone who is in a position to affect the employee's tenure, status, or compensation with the organization. Thus, when an employee is asked for a date or perhaps something more explicitly sexual by someone who is not able to influence the employee's conditions of employment, and it is not done in an offensive, hostile, or intimidating manner, no sexual harassment takes place. Most employers realize that it is impossible to place normal men and women together on the job without sexual fraternization taking place almost immediately. Fraternization among peers, however, does not constitute sexual harassment, except if it becomes overly intimidating, hostile, or offensive to the affected individual.

However, employers should be very cautious of any sexual fraternization where one partner outranks the other within the organizational hierarchy. These situations represent serious threats that litigation will eventually ensue and need to be addressed as a matter of mandatory company policy. Employers will find, if necessary by bitter experience, that sexual harassment is one area where policies have to be strictly defined and rigidly enforced, sometimes with extreme prejudice toward individuals who cannot comply and thereby threaten the organization with potentially dire legal consequences.

Employers must make it known to supervisors and managers that sexual fraternization with subordinates, no matter how innocent it may seem to them, will not be tolerated. Admittedly, the law only outlaws *unwelcome* advances by superiors toward subordinates, and only if these unwelcome advances are meant to influence the terms and conditions of the subordinate's employment. But how is the employer to prove lack of improper motive later on in court?

The law attaches a great deal of weight and validity to the subordinate's implicit understanding of the superior's motive in subjecting the subordinate to sexual advances, in determining whether sexual harassment has taken place. This is true even if the superior is able to plead truthfully that his or her motives were purely above-board as far as trading sex for some sort of preferential treatment was concerned.

Sexual harassment in the form of subjecting an employee to an intimidating, hostile, or offensive work environment is a particularly difficult area for employers, given that any male employee is capable of directing such conduct toward any female employee, regardless of their respective places within the organizational hierarchy. Superiors can harass subordinates; subordinates can harass superiors and coworkers can harass coworkers.

Although it is presumably not within the scope of a supervisor's or manager's explicit authority to commit acts of sexual harassment toward subordinates, the law will consider any such acts of a supervisor or manager toward subordinates as being the acts of the employer. Vicarious liability will be assigned to the employer, whether the employer is an individual, partnership, or corporation.

The employer may have a defense, however, to acts of sexual harassment which create an intimidating, hostile, or offensive work environment, and do not involve sex as a term or condition or employment, which occur on the same level of organizational rank or which are directed backward in the chain of command. The defense is only valid if the employer has satisfied its duty to take preventative measures with respect to such conduct, and the employer or appropriate individuals within the chain of command are not actually aware that it is taking place.

It also deserves mentioning that no individual is immune to the legal consequences of his or her own behavior, whether or not a higher manager or supervisor, partner, corporate officer, corporate director, or the corporation itself is also responsible for the individual's conduct on principles of vicarious legal liability. The complex nuances which come into play in these situations are discussed in more detail in Chapter 5 of this book dealing with organizational risk management.

Employers have the obligation to take affirmative action to see that sexual harassment of both general types does not occur in the workplace. Employers have to educate not only supervisors and managers as to their special responsibilities, but also have to instruct the rank and file as to what sexual harassment is and assure both potential victims and potential perpetrators of intimidating, hostile, and offensive sexual behavior that such harassment directed at others will not be tolerated. Furthermore, employers must set up viable procedures to insure that victims can bring their complaints to management for a fair hearing, and employers must demonstrate forcefully and effectively that actual acts of harassment will not go unpunished.

Other Requirements That Claimant Must Demonstrate

Whether or not management will be responsible for what has happened, the courts have set out an additional potential defense to sexual harassment of the intimidating, hostile, or offensive work environment variety. State and federal courts generally require for such a case to succeed that the affected individual must show that his or her psychological well-being has been seriously affected or that he or she has been made to suffer to the point where the work environment has become intolerable.

The courts in different jurisdictions phrase it differently, but the point is that there is a threshold of seriousness the claimant must overcome before his or her case will be compensable at all. That threshold is meant to be sufficiently high enough that only very serious, intimidating, hostile, or offensive work environment cases will receive a hearing in court or be eligible for any measure of compensation whatsoever.

This is different from other civil litigation, where very small cases might receive very little compensation, for example in small claims court, while larger cases are worth correspondingly larger amounts. It is also different from discrimination cases in other contexts, where the consequences of discrimination are to be rectified no matter how trivial they may seem to others who are not members of minorities who have traditionally had to endure unequal treatment without legal recourse.

Whether or not the threshold for compensable sexual harassment of the intimidating, hostile, or offensive work environment variety has been met is determined not by the actual reaction the particular disaffected individual bringing the case has experienced, but the reaction an individual of average temperament and sensibilities would be expected to experience under the same or similar set of circumstances. Often as a practical matter the claimant must bring expert evidence from a psychological or psychiatric professional, not only to substantiate the actual reaction he or she will claim to have undergone, but also to place his or her reaction in its proper perspective in relation to the reaction the average, normal person would be expected to undergo if exposed to the same treatment.

Considerations of Claimant

Once the courtroom door has been opened to the psychological or psychiatric professions, and the case has become a battle of expert witnesses in the mental health professions, the disaffected party can be in for a profoundly rancorous and distasteful experience which can rival or even surpass the events which brought the case to the courtroom in the first place. Mental health professionals can with impunity dredge up and bring out any real, imagined, or surmised fact from an individual's past in support of a psychological assessment or psychiatric diagnosis which tends to take the blame for an individual's problems away from the employer's or coworker's conduct by placing elsewhere in the individual's psychic history or emotional profile.

An individual may instigate a claim, from the employee's perspective, with an honestly deserved air of righteous indignation, or from the employer's perspective only with a lust for the undeserved spoils of litigation. Either way, the individual will eventually learn that when the state of his or her mental health is brought into question, either by his or her claims to have suffered as the result of the employer's wrongful conduct, or by the employer as an alleged motive for filing a compensation claim, the whole matter likely will eventually turn very ugly and sordid. The affected individual may decide that in the long run the case is not worth pursuing, no matter how valid the claim might be.

Unfortunately, many disaffected individuals and their legal counsel underestimate just how awful an experience the actual litigation of a sexual harassment claim can become. Knowledgeable employer defendants can exploit this to their advantage, rightfully or wrongly. There is usually a limit to how much any given individual can tolerate probing interrogation on the defense psychiatrist's couch, seemingly endless rounds of in-depth psychological testing, and insulting and demeaning labelling by defense mental health professionals, perhaps in open court in front of their family, friends, and sympathetic coworkers. Defensive strategies in these cases often end up relying on tactics of this nature, often to the eventual detriment of the court's and both sides' sensibilities.

Protection of claimants is difficult. The courts have no way to know in advance which parties have meritorious claims and do not deserve to be subjected to distasteful probing and labelling and which are bringing unmeritorious causes which deserve to be exposed as such. Thus, the courts will usually give defendants in sexual harassment claims a free hand under court rules and statutes which permit independent medical and psychiatric examinations of parties to litigation. The courts will also permit comprehensive interrogation of parties as to their sexual, family, and work histories and will allow very rigorous and thorough cross-examination of any mental health professionals who have or are treating the disaffected individual bringing the claim.

These cases are usually won or lost on the basis of the amount of grit and endurance the disaffected party brings with to get through the struggle, rather than the actual merits of the claim. Whether this is right or wrong, everyone involved needs to understand that it is a fact of life in sexual harassment claims that no one really ever wins.

Employers should not wait until a claim comes before an administrative agency or is filed in court to take action where sexual harassment is concerned. These cases are enormously expensive, even to win, when attorney fees and litigation costs are fully accounted for. Even more important for employers to consider are the intangible costs in lost productivity and drained organizational morale if employers are not able to implement effective policies from the start. Outside consultants are available to help where in-house resources are lacking and often provide a cost-effective use of organizational resources.

It should be pointed out that although the victims of sexual harassment are typically women, and the perpetrators are typically men, there is nothing in the law which says that it cannot happen the other way around. Further, it can be envisioned that persons of the same gender as the victim could participate in making the work environment intimidating, hostile, or offensive from a sexual standpoint, by participating in vulgar or offensive sexually-oriented conduct directed at the sensibilities of a particular victim.

It is also conceivable that sexual harassment of either of the two basic types could take on homosexual overtones. This could happen with a homosexual supervisor or manager attempting to seduce a same-gender homosexual or same-gender heterosexual partner by making that individual's employment prospects contingent on his or her acquiescence. Or an individual could be selected for intimidating, hostile, or offensive treatment with homosexual or heterosexual overtones because the individual's sexual preference contrasts with the prevailing orientation of other individuals in the workplace. It is not known definitively how any of these particular scenarios would be decided by the courts, but there is no reason to believe that the homosexual nature of the situation would make any difference.

Conclusion

The law of sexual harassment should give sober and responsible employers more than ample pause to think how their operations can be interrupted and financial statements affected by claims of this nature.

Chapter Sixteen

Marital Status Discrimination

Marital status discrimination is now illegal under federal law and the antidiscrimination or civil rights laws of about half of the states. The law in this area is an outgrowth of Title VII of the Civil Rights Act of 1964, a comprehensive federal statute designed to outlaw discrimination in employment and in many other facets of our national life. In general, Title VII only applies to employers in the private and public sectors with fifteen or more employees for each working day in each of twenty or more calendar weeks in the current or preceding calendar year. State laws, where applicable, tend to apply to all employers in the state, regardless of size, and to state and municipal governmental entities as well.

Originally, the law only made it illegal for employers to discriminate in employment decisions against individuals on the basis of gender, unless the gender of the employee in question could be shown to be a bona fide or good faith occupational qualification for the job which was reasonably necessary to the employer's business operations. The law said nothing about marital status as a forbidden criterion of employment discrimination.

In actual practice, however, the Equal Employment Opportunity Commission, which enforces the employment antidiscrimination provisions of Title VII of the 1964 Civil Rights Act, found that marital status was a frequently-encountered factor in what was termed "sex-plus" discrimination. "Sex-plus" discrimination occurred where women who possessed a certain attribute were treated differently in the workplace from men with the same condition. Or more simply, married women were being treated differently than married men were treated, and thus were being discriminated against contrary to the intent of Title VII of the Civil Rights Act. Given this situation, the EEOC used its rule-making authority to put regulations into effect that held discrimination against married women was a form of gender-based discrimination forbidden by Title VII of the Civil Rights Act.

Ground-Breaking Cases

The first cases to break ground in court over this issue were the flight attendant cases filed in the late 1960s and early 1970s. Airlines typically only hired unmarried women as flight attendants and required women to resign when they became engaged or at least by the time they actually married. Male flight attendants were hired and permitted to keep their jobs regardless of their marital status. The courts uniformly ruled that marital status was an impermissible basis for employment-related decisions and struck down no-marriage rules for flight attendants throughout the airline industry.

These cases reflected a new legal development—the passage of Title VII and the implementation of the EEOC's policy against marital status discrimination. These cases also reflected a changing consciousness in our society about the roles of men and women in the workplace. Women in the workplace, particularly younger women in highly visible service positions, were no longer there to create an illusion of sexual availability for their employers and employer's customers, which would be tarnished by their commitment to the state of marriage. They were there to do their particular jobs, jobs which could be done by competent unmarried women, married women, unmarried men, or married men regardless of the status of their private sexual and family lives. Women who were married could be expected to become pregnant and to take time away from the job for family concerns, but that would be a matter of individual choice rather than of categorical prejudice as to the proper place of married women in our society.

After the flight attendants won their cases and won the right to keep their jobs regardless of their marital status preference, a great deal of other litigation during the mid and latter 1970s and early 1980s. It concerned how the airlines would remedy the effects of past discrimination. The courts had to wrestle with cases filed by flight attendants who had resigned or been forced out perhaps ten or fifteen years earlier. Those flight attendants argued in court that they not only wanted to return to work, but they would have stayed on the whole time had there been no antimarriage rules at the companies where they had been employed.

The courts had to decide whether to award back pay, one of the usual remedies in favor of parties who have been excluded from the workplace by employer discriminatory policies and conduct. The courts also had to weigh how to balance the remedial seniority rights of displaced workers with the seniority rights of those who had not married and had stayed on with the airlines through the whole time or those who had been hired or had been married after the airlines changed their antidiscriminatory policies.

Obviously, when an employer engages in discriminatory conduct and is later called to task in court or before an administrative body on the federal or state level, and discrimination can be proven, the job of remedying the effects of discrimination will be very costly. It will be necessary to place past victims in the same place they would have been had no discrimination taken place.

Fortunately, the issues in the cases which had to remedy the effects of past marital status discrimination are now a moot point. Most, employers got the message in the late 1960s or early 1970s and no longer discriminate.

It is still of the utmost importance, however, for employers to be able to recognize marital status discrimination and not to engage in it. Most of the present cases do not involve outright bans on hiring or retaining the services of married women, since this is almost universally recognized as an inappropriate practice, but involve more subtle manifestations of marital status discrimination.

Antinepotism Rules

One area which still receives a fair amount of attention are the problems encountered with employer antinepotism rules. Nepotism is the practice of granting favors to close relatives. Many employers realize the adverse effects nepotism can have upon organizational morale and efficient functioning of the enterprise when it is allowed to enter into personnel decisions. Some employers have instigated rules which forbid the hiring of certain close relatives of existing employees anywhere in the company, or, with larger companies, forbid close relatives to work with each other or, especially, to supervise each other in the same branch or division of the company.

Employer rules which will discriminate against someone on the basis of that person being the son or daughter, niece or nephew, or aunt or uncle of an existing employee are permissible as long as the rules do not apply unevenly to one gender over the other. Rules against husbands and wives working too closely together are sanctioned by the law, as long as they do not favor one spouse over the other.

Husbands and Wives

The situation involving husbands and wives is different than others in that two individuals might not be related when they come to work. They may meet, become engaged, and decide to marry each other while both are employed by the same company which forbids them to work together after they take their vows.

It is perfectly permissible to require a husband or a wife to leave the company or to transfer to another division after wedlock. This is true under Title VII of the Civil Rights Act of 1964 and the EEOC antidiscrimination guidelines, as long as no preference is imposed by the employer, overtly or subtly, as to who is to stay and who is to leave. State law in some jurisdictions, however, may indicate otherwise.

In actual practice it is not so simple, because there have been situations in which application of no-spouse rules, neutral on the face of it, have so strongly favored husbands that the courts have been willing to find discrimination to have occurred by applying rules of "disparate impact" analysis. Remember that the purpose of antidiscrimination law relative to marital status is designed to address society's once widely held prejudice that the place of married women is in the home. The courts will be suspicious whenever there is a situation which operates against women or any other protected "minority" group, even if the situation doesn't exist as a result of explicit employer policy or overt practice. The courts may even be willing to rule that discrimination is going on just on the basis that the minority group is affected on a disparate basis compared to the majority.

Where enforcement of company no-spouse rules have led to a disproportionate percentage of wives resigning in favor of their husbands keeping their jobs, the EEOC, state fair employment commissions, and the courts are likely to conclude that there is some form of subtle pressure going on to force women out of the workplace. They may decide that marital status discrimination is taking place despite the existence of a facially neutral employer policy on the issue.

It is not enough just to assume that husbands and wives recognize that the husband is the one who should have the career and that the wife's central sphere of responsibility lies elsewhere, because that thinking is the sort of outdated bias the law was meant to cure. It may be, in fact, that couples have been making their decisions on the basis that the woman's job pays less, is less prestigious, or is not on the track to supervision or upper management. Digging into concerns over the disparate impact of the company's no-spouse rule may only reveal a much more profound degree of gender-based discrimination in the organizational structure.

Some companies have similar rules which forbid employment within the company of spouses of competing business concerns. As long as these policies do not explicitly or even implicitly favor one gender over the other, they are permissible. That is, wives whose husbands work for competitors have to be treated the same as husbands whose wives are employed by competing companies. Administrative agencies and the courts will look not only at the employer's stated policy, but at the actual enforcement of the policy to be sure that such a policy does not have a differential impact on one gender over the other.

State Laws

Nearly all of the states have a civil rights, human rights, or fair employment statute. About half of these explicitly outlaw marital status discrimination. Most of the states which do expressly outlaw marital status discrimination follow federal law for their definition of just what marital status discrimination entails. However, a minority of states have read their own laws against marital status discrimination to forbid no-spouse rules on the job, whether an expression of the employer's antinepotism policy was put in place for some other reason. In these states, it is illegal simply to discriminate on the basis of whether or not someone is married, but also to discriminate on the basis that the person is married or chooses to get married to someone who is a co-worker, subordinate, or superior.

Although the number of states which follow this interpretation of the law is very small, it is still necessary for every business owner, executive, and human resources manager to become familiar with state law on the subject. Policies and practices which are permissible on the federal level may run afoul of state law. As indicated in Chapter 9 of this book on general considerations relative to antidiscrimination law, the states are free to enact and to implement their own rules on discrimination, just as long as those rules do not attempt to relax the provisions of federal law, but are at least as stringent or more stringent with the subject than the federal authorities have chosen to be.

Although it is not covered anywhere in the EEOC regulations, employers should assume that discrimination against men on the basis of their marital status would be illegal. Employers presumably cannot discriminate against women on this basis and would be treating men differently based on their gender if they were able to discriminate against them. Discrimination against unmarried women in favor of married women would also probably be struck down, although the EEOC regulations do not explicitly say so.

Marital status discrimination is illegal regardless of who benefits by it. Even if another woman, albeit unmarried, stands to benefit from an employer policy or practice which discriminates against married women, the policy or practice is illegal. It does not have to be unmarried or married men who benefit from a particular married woman's disadvantaged status to render the policy which produces that disadvantaged status illegal.

One other practice which has been struck down is the practice of hiring married "teams" for certain jobs like residential apartment management positions. It is not permissible to insist that a "team" consist of two individuals married to each other, but an employer can, if the exigencies of the job situation call for it, insist on hiring two individuals who are willing to live and work closely together, rather than two separate persons who are not so inclined. Thus, close friends or even same-gender gay lovers have the same opportunity in these situations.

Even though marital status has been ruled illegal throughout the economy, the EEOC and most state laws have left open the possibility that there will be "bona fide occupational qualifications" which will permit differential treatment to exist based on marital status. The only problem has been finding circumstances where such a bona fide or good faith qualification actually exists. Antinepotism rules were once held up as an example of a bona fide occupational qualification, but these rules cannot actually be allowed to operate against a married woman or in favor of a married man.

Conclusion

The only safe assumption is that there now are no circumstances where true marital status discrimination will be tolerated, whether it means discrimination against married women in favor of unmarried women or in favor of married or unmarried men. All employers must stamp out this once widespread practice and should take steps to educate lower and middle-level supervisors and managers as to how marital status bias, based on outmoded views of the proper social and familial roles of married women, can manifest itself in how certain employees are treated.

Chapter Seventeen

Pregnancy Discrimination

As discussed elsewhere in this book, Title VII of the Civil Rights Act of 1964 is the principal federal law standing behind a firm national policy in this country intended to outlaw discrimination in employment. Many states and a few local municipal jurisdictions also have laws which regulate the general subject of discrimination in employment, but the focus in this chapter is on federal law because most applicable state laws do not differ significantly from federal law with respect to the subjects of pregnancy and pregnancy-benefits discrimination.

Title VII, which is codified in the United States Code at Title 42, Section 2000e-2, states that it is an unlawful employment practice for an employer to fail or refuse to hire or to discharge any individual, or otherwise to discriminate against any individual with respect to compensation, terms, conditions, or privileges of employment because of the individual's race, color, religion, sex or national origin. As originally, enacted Title VII did not specifically deal with pregnancy as a factor in unlawful sex or gender-based discrimination. However, under the authority delegated to it by Congress, the Equal Employment Opportunity Commission early on put guidelines into effect setting forth the EEOC's interpretation of Title VII. The interpretation was that discrimination in employment with respect to pregnancy itself or availability of benefits for pregnancy-related conditions does amount to a violation of the laws meant to outlaw gender-based discrimination. The EEOC guidelines on employment policies relating to pregnancy and childbirth can be found in the code at Title 29, Section 1604.10.

Title VII and the EEOC guidelines apply only to private and public-sector employers with fifteen or more employees for each working day in each of twenty or more calendar weeks in the current or preceding calendar year. State laws, where applicable, generally apply to all employers in the state, including state and local government.

Supreme Court Rulings

Although the law has been subsequently clarified to a great extent, a good deal of confusion entered the picture in 1976 when the Supreme Court of the United States ruled in the *Gilbert* v. *General Electric Co.* (429 U.S. 125, 50 L. Ed. 2d 343, 97 S. Ct. 401) case that the EEOC had stepped outside the bounds of its authority and was incorrect in issuing guidelines which held that pregnancy discrimination in employment was a form of gender-based discrimination which Congress had outlawed by passage of the gender-discrimination provisions of Title VII of the 1964 Civil Rights Act.

The Supreme Court had earlier ruled in 1974 in *Geduldig* v. *Aiello* (417 U.S. 484, 41 L. Ed. 2d 256, 94 S. Ct. 2485) that there was no basis under the Fourteenth Amendment to the Constitution for ruling that gender-based discrimination was unconstitutional. The Supreme Court ruled that the Fourteenth Amendment simply was not meant to cover the subject of gender-based discrimination and could not be stretched by the process of judicial interpretation to encompass this subject.

With these two rulings, the Supreme Court effectively said there was no federal law standing in the way of pregnancy discrimination in the workplace. In the two years following *Gilbert* v. *General Electric Co.*, lower courts began revising their decisions. The EEOC did a complete about face on the issue and private and public employers who wished to do so were able to revise their policies substantially in this area. Then Congress made it clear with the passage of the 1978 amendments to Title VII of the Civil Rights Act of 1964 contained in the Pregnancy Discrimination Act of 1978, effective April 1979, that pregnancy discrimination was a facet of gender-based discrimination it had meant to outlaw with the original passage of Title VII.

Congress explicitly approved the EEOC guidelines, which the Supreme Court had thrown out as contrary to the intent of Congress, by writing the guidelines almost verbatim into Title VII of the Civil Rights Act. Since *Gilbert* v. *General Electric Co.* had been based on the Supreme Court's reading of Congress' intent in enacting Title VII, and Congress now had passed a law plainly stating that the Supreme Court's reading of Congress' intent had been wrong and stating what Congress' intent was, the *Gilbert* v. *General Electric Co.* decision was effectively overruled.

After 1978, the picture remained unclear because it was still necessary for the courts to try to decide what the law had been for acts of discrimination occurring between 1974 and 1978, a relatively short but highly active period in the development of the law of employment discrimination. The courts had to rethink decisions handed down during this period, which had overturned previous rulings of law which after 1978 turned out had been right all along. Needless to say, the court decisions remained very difficult to follow for a considerable period of time even after Congress made a definitive statement on the subject of pregnancy discrimination in 1978.

The point of this very technical discussion of legal history has been to alert business owners, managers, and executives and personnel professionals to the fact there has been a great deal of confusing and contradictory material published on the subject of pregnancy discrimination growing out of the state of the law during the time between the *Geduldig* v. *Aiello* decision in 1974, *Gilbert* v. *General Electric Co.* in 1976, and the 1978 amendments to Title VII of the Civil Rights Act contained in the Pregnancy Discrimination Act of 1978.

EEOC's Guidelines

Now it is clear that the EEOC's guidelines on pregnancy-based discrimination in employment and employment benefits are once again the law of the land. Thus, it is very important for employers to have some level of familiarity with the basic premises behind these regulations and understand how the guidelines are being interpreted in the courts.

First of all, it is illegal under the EEOC guidelines to exclude applicants or employees from employment because of pregnancy, unless the employer can demonstrate that not being pregnant represents a bona fide occupational qualification. A bona fide occupational qualification, in general terms, means that the employer can, in good faith, demonstrate an objective reason why a pregnant person cannot do the job because of her pregnancy.

This will usually only exclude or permit pregnancy-based exclusions from the workplace of women in jobs which demand levels of physical agility which are significantly compromised by pregnancy, like the airline flight attendants whose cases are discussed later in this chapter. It is important that exclusions because of pregnancy not amount to what are now considered merely outmoded and grossly inappropriate prejudices directed at pregnant women.

The laws against every form of discrimination are meant to correct outmoded social stereotypes which arbitrarily restrict the access of certain classes of affected individuals to full employment opportunity. Employers must carefully search their motives in formulating policies and practices dealing with pregnancy to see that their policies and practices really pertain to objective performance factors and the demands of the job and do not merely reflect the feelings of certain individuals that pregnant women perhaps do not belong anywhere but at home or show an unwillingness by some to accommodate the changes in appearance which accompany pregnancy in its latter stages. If the employer's conduct is based on bias rather than objective factors, the employer is certain to be challenged before the EEOC or in court at some point in time.

In general, it is very unlikely that any exclusion of women from hiring or from continued employment for being pregnant will stand up as a legitimate bona fide occupational qualification. This is especially true in view of employers' responsibilities under the EEOC guidelines with respect to making medical benefits and maternity leave available for pregnancy-related conditions.

Most of the administrative proceedings and civil court cases involving pregnancy as a factor in job discrimination have focused on the second major area covered by the EEOC guidelines, which is how pregnancy, childbirth, and related medical conditions must be treated as disabilities for purposes of health and disability insurance and sick leave policies. Related areas of concern are termination from employment due to insufficient maternity leave being available to cover absence from work due to pregnancy-related conditions, and how time off for pregnancy and delivery are handled with respect to job seniority.

Nowhere in Title VII or the EEOC guidelines are employers explicitly required to make health insurance, disability benefits, or sick or maternity leave available to anyone, including pregnant women, women suffering from medical conditions associated with pregnancy or childbirth, or, for that matter, to the men in their lives. However, as we will see, the practical effect of the EEOC guidelines, which have the same force and effect as other federal regulatory law, is to require employers to make these benefits available under many circumstances to women affected by pregnancy-related conditions.

The important operative language in the EEOC guidelines is that pregnancy, childbirth, or related medical conditions must be treated by the employer "on the same terms and conditions" as other disabilities for purposes of policies and practices involving leave, seniority, benefits, reinstatement, and payments under health or disability insurance and sick leave plans. This means just what it says. If the employer has any sort of sick leave, medical leave, personal leave, annual leave, medical insurance, disability insurance, and the like, it must apply in all particulars exactly the same to pregnancy as it does to other conditions. Seniority on the job can be affected by time off for pregnancy or pregnancy-related conditions only in exactly the same fashion as seniority is affected by other disabilities which require or allow the employee to be away from work.

The EEOC guidelines have been amended in some particulars over the past two decades, to clarify the position of Congress and the EEOC in response to court decisions which have interpreted the guidelines contrary to the policies which the Congress and the EEOC intended to bring into effect, and more generally in response to changing political conditions in this country.

In the main, the overall import of the regulations has not changed, except during the 1974 to 1978 period discussed above. However, the EEOC guidelines have changed materially over the years on the abortion issue. On the abortion issue, as presently written, the EEOC guidelines explicitly state, as an exception to the general rule, that no employer is required to provide health insurance benefits for abortion, except where the life of the mother would be endangered if the fetus were carried to term or where medical complications have arisen from an abortion.

However, employers are in no way precluded by the language of the EEOC guidelines from providing health insurance or other benefits with respect to abortion, whether or not the mother's life or health is in jeopardy.

One other technicality embodied in the EEOC guidelines is that the guidelines apply whether or not the employer's policy covering pregnancy and childbirth benefits is incorporated into a collective bargaining agreement. This provision of the guidelines has the effect of insuring that the subject of pregnancy, childbirth, and maternity benefits is kept out of the realm of labor law and dealt with only as a matter of antidiscrimination policies subject to EEOC jurisdiction.

Leading Cases Which Interpreted the Law

One of the early leading cases interpreting the law in this area treated the question whether Title VII and the EEOC guidelines dealt with benefits for normal pregnancies, or only required benefits to be paid with respect to medical complications arising from difficult or abnormal pregnancies or births.

The employer in that case had a sick leave policy under which full-time employees were able to take leave with pay for a wide range of non-job-related conditions, up to their accumulated sick-leave balance, and to suffer no adverse consequences with respect to seniority, opportunities for promotion, and accumulation of pension benefits and vacation time during or after a leave of absence was sanctioned by the employer's sick leave policy. Sick leave could be used for medical conditions unique to only one sex, such as prostate operations for men and miscarriages or abortions for women, so it was not possible to find that the employer's policies discriminated in other respects on the basis of the gender of the affected employee.

However, under the employer's policy, sick leave could not be used for "normal" uncomplicated pregnancy and childbirth. But if a woman was off on uncompensated leave and happened to experience abnormal complications, she could apply for and receive sick leave benefits to the extent her continued absence was due to these extenuating factors. The import of the case was to challenge in court the employer's policy only as it pertained to maternity leave necessitated by "normal" uncomplicated pregnancy and childbirth.

Title VII and, more directly, the EEOC guidelines on employer pregnancy and childbirth benefit policies were the deciding factor in the court's decision to strike down the employer's sick leave policy in this case as illegal insofar as it excluded maternity leave occasioned by "normal" uncomplicated pregnancy from its sick leave policy.

Congress gave authority to the EEOC to implement the well-articulated national policy against employment discrimination which is embodied in Title VII, by issuing guidelines which have the force and effect of law as federal regulations binding on all employers. The policy was in effect regardless of whether other parties, governmental bodies, or the courts might think that denial of pregnancy, childbirth, and maternity leave benefits in normal circumstances did not constitute unlawful sex or gender-based discrimination.

The court also rejected the argument which had surfaced in other litigated cases that it was permissible for employers to make the availability of sick leave, disability, and health insurance benefits contingent on the "voluntariness" of the medical or health-related condition for which payment was sought. Pregnancy was to be treated as any other temporary disability, without splitting hairs over moral, physiological, or psychological questions concerning its volitional basis.

Cost to the employer of making benefits available for pregnancy was not an objection which the court could consider as a defense to compliance with the EEOC guidelines. Cost simply is not and never has been a valid legal basis for refusal to implement anti-discrimination policies directly mandated by Title VII.

Another instructive case, which helps to define the outer boundary of the employer's responsibilities in this area, involved a woman with what was described as a sit-down, clerical job. The employer's policy was to grant any employee up to five months leave with pay for illness or injury, regardless of the nature of the condition or the gender of the employee.

The individual employee in question was told by her manager she would receive four weeks leave for delivery of her baby, which was her second child and proved to be unremarkable from a medical standpoint. If there was demonstrated need for it, the manager could extend her leave with pay an additional two weeks. After these first six weeks, the decision went to the department head, and then later to the president of the company, whether the employee would be granted up to a total of five months off with pay. Employees were expected to return to work on light duty if able to do only light duties.

The affected employee obtained a letter from her doctor stating that the employee wished to be off with pay an additional two weeks beyond the four weeks originally offered. Her manager declined to grant her this additional paid leave, on the basis that there was no demonstrated medical reason for her to remain off work that long following the birth of her child.

The court upheld the manager's conduct and the employer's policies in this case with regard to benefits for "pregnancy, childbirth, and related medical conditions" as set out in the EEOC guidelines, even praising the company for its enlightened, liberal attention to its employees' legitimate needs and its evenhanded application of its leave policies.

It was crucial to the court's decision to uphold to the company that leave was available on the same terms and conditions without regard to the nature of the condition for which it was sought, and

Index

A

Abortion, and pregnancy discrimination, 168
Administrative agencies, 93–94
Age discrimination, 101–108
Age Discrimination in Employment Act, 89, 101–104
Affirmative action,
  and race discrimination, 131
  and sex discrimination, 141, 142–143
AIDS, 90
Alcohol testing, 67–77
Americans With Disabilities Act of 1990, 89, 109–111, 113
Applications for employment, and age discrimination, 105
Atheism, and religious discrimination, 120
At will, employment, 2–4, 69
Attorneys fees, 12, 57, 95

B

Benefits, and sex discrimination, 139
Black Muslim faith, and religious discrimination, 120

Bona fide occupational requirements,
  and age discrimination, 106–107
  and sex discrimination, 140
Breath analysis, alcohol, 75

C

Christmas, and religious discrimination, 123
Civil Rights Act of 1964, 89, 119–120, 128, 136–137, 146, 155–156, 158, 163–165
Collective bargaining, 3, 70–71
Common law employee at will, 2–4, 69
Complaints to public agencies, 15–16
Copyright, 34
Corporations, 46
Constitutional rights, 71–73
Constructive termination, 5

D

Damage awards,
  for defamation, 29
  for discrimination, 94–95

for retaliatory discharge, 11–12
for sexual harassment, 148
Defamation, 22–24
Defend, duty to, 50–51
Disability discrimination,
    in general, 109–117
    and state law, 114–117
Discharge, retaliatory, 11–20
Disciplinary procedures, 7–8
Discrimination, in general, 89–99
Dismissal, 24
Disparate impact,
    in race discrimination, 130–131
    in sex discrimination, 140–142
Dress and grooming standards, 123–124
Drug testing, 67–77, 113

E

Easter, and religious discrimination, 123
Emotional distress, 12, 86–87
Employee at will, 2–4, 14–15, 69
Equal Employment Opportunity Commission (EEOC),
    92–94, 96, 103–105, 107, 113,
    126, 129–132, 139, 141, 145–146, 158–161, 163–173

F

Federal pre-emption, 91

G

Gilbert v. *General Electric Co.*,
    164–165
Geduldig v. *Aiello*, 164–165

H

Handbooks, employee, 1–10
Help wanted ads,
    and age discrimination, 104–105
    and sex discrimination, 138

I

Indemnify, duty to, 51–53
Industrial insurance, 13–14
Insurance coverage, 49
Intentional misconduct, 48, 63–65
Interstate Commerce Clause,
    91, 110

J

Jury duty, 17
Just cause for termination, 5–8

K

Ku Klux Klan and religious discrimination, 120

L

Liability insurance, 53–54

Libel, 22
Limited partnerships, 46

M

Mandatory retirement, 105–106
Marital status discrimination, 155–161
Maternity benefits, 139
Medical examinations, 112–113
Mental anguish, 12
Military reserves, 17

N

Negligence, 47–48, 62–63
Nepotism, 158
Noncompetition agreements, 31–41
Non-smokers' rights, 81–82

O

Objective criteria, 97–99
Off the job conduct, 68–69, 80
Office of Federal Contract Compliance guidelines, 120

P

Partnerships, 44–45
Passover, and religious discrimination, 123
Patents, 33–34
Prayer on the job, 125
Pregnancy discrimination, 163–173

Pregnancy Discrimination Act of 1978, 165
Privileged communication, 26–27
Proselytizing, religious, 124–125
Punitive damages, 12, 65, 95

R

Race discrimination, 127–134
Reasonable accommodation, and disability discrimination, 112
and religious discrimination, 121–122
Rehabilitation Act of 1973, 109–110
Religious discrimination, 119–126
Retaliatory discharge, 11–20
Retirement, mandatory, 105–106
Records, personnel, 19, 21–30, 112–113, 130–131
Risk management, 43–56
Rosh Hashanah, and religious discrimination, 123

S

Sabbath observance, and religious discrimination, 121–123
Screening, drug and alcohol, 67–68
Sex discrimination, 135–143

Sexual harassment, 135, 145–
    154
Slander, 22
Smoking, 79–88
Sole proprietorships, 44
Stress, 57–66
Surveillance of employees, 76

T

Title VII, 89, 128, 136–137, 139,
    146, 155–156, 158, 163–165,
    167–171
Trademarks, 34

U

Undue hardship,
  and disability discrimination,
    112
  and religious discrimination,
    121–123
Uniform Guidelines on Em-
    ployee Selection Proce-
    dures, 131–133

V

Vicarious liability,
  in general, 46
  for sexual harassment, 150
Voting, time off for, 17

W

Waiver of liability, 24
"Whistle blowing," 17–18

Workers' compensation, 13–14,
    54–56, 58–62, 84–86
Wrongful discharge. *See* retalia-
    tory discharge

Additional Titles in
The Entrepreneur's Guide Series
Available from Probus Publishing

How to Sell Your Business for the Best Price, Vaughn Cox

Entrepreneur's Guide to Capital, Revised Edition, Jennifer Lindsey

Cashflow, Credit and Collection, Basil P. Mavrovitis

Mastering the Business Cycle, Albert N. Link

Negotiating a Bank Loan, Arthur G. Pulis III

Crafting the Perfect Name, George Burroughs Blake and Nancy Blake-Bohné

Acquisitions, Sharon L. Blanding

Telemarketing That Works, Raymond C. Harlan and Walter M. Woolfson, Jr.

Building a Winning Sales Team, Gini Graham Scott

Forthcoming Titles

Developing a Company Policy Manual, Michael Reaves, Available in October 1991

Short-Term Money, Jeff Madura, E. Theodore Veit and Daniel E. McCarty, Available in November 1991

How to Export, Roger Fritz, Available in December 1991